GRASPING LEGAL TIME

Time is one of the most important means for the exercise of power. In migration law, it is used for disciplining and controlling the presence of migrants within a certain territory through the intricate interplay of two overlapping but contradicting understandings of time – human and clock time. This book explores both the success and limitations of the usage of time for the governance of migration. The virtues of legal time can be seen at work in several temporal differentiations in migration law: differentiation based on temporality, deadlines, qualification of time and procedural differentiation. Martijn Stronks contests that, hidden in the usage of legal time in migration law, there is an argument for the inclusion of migrants on the basis of their right to human time. This assertion is based in the finite, irreversible and unstoppable character of human time.

MARTIJN STRONKS is an assistant professor at the Amsterdam Centre for Migration and Refugee Law of the Vrije Universiteit Amsterdam. He studied law and philosophy at the Vrije Universiteit Amsterdam and the University of Cape Town. His main research interests include migration and human rights law, legal philosophy, and time.

CAMBRIDGE ASYLUM AND MIGRATION STUDIES

At no time in modern history have so many people been on the move as at present. Migration facilitates critical social, economic, and humanitarian linkages. But it may also challenge prevailing notions of bounded political communities, of security, and of international law.

The political and legal systems that regulate the transborder movement of persons were largely devised in the mid-twentieth century, and are showing their strains. New challenges have arisen for policymakers, advocates, and decision-makers that require the adaptation and evolution of traditional models to meet emerging imperatives.

Edited by a world leader in refugee law, this new series aims to be a forum for innovative writing on all aspects of the transnational movement of people. It publishes single or coauthored works that may be legal, political, or cross-disciplinary in nature, and will be essential reading for anyone looking to understand one of the most important issues of the twenty-first century

Books in the Series

The Child in International Refugee Law Jason M. Pobjoy

Refuge Lost: Asylum Law in an Interdependent World Daniel Ghezelbash

Demanding Rights: Europe's Supranational Courts and the Dilemma of Migrant Vulnerability Moritz Baumgärtel

Climate Change, Disasters, and the Refugee Convention Matthew Scott

The Global Governed?: Refugees as Providers of Protection and Assistance Kate Pincock, Alexander Betts and Evan Easton-Calabria

The Evolution of Humanitarian Protection in European Law and Practice Liv Feijen

Protection from Refuge: From Refugee Rights to Migration Management Kate Ogg

GRASPING LEGAL TIME

Temporality and European Migration Law

MARTIJN STRONKS
Vrije Universiteit Amsterdam

CAMBRIDGE
UNIVERSITY PRESS

CAMBRIDGE
UNIVERSITY PRESS

Shaftesbury Road, Cambridge CB2 8EA, United Kingdom

One Liberty Plaza, 20th Floor, New York, NY 10006, USA

477 Williamstown Road, Port Melbourne, VIC 3207, Australia

314–321, 3rd Floor, Plot 3, Splendor Forum, Jasola District Centre, New Delhi – 110025, India

103 Penang Road, #05–06/07, Visioncrest Commercial, Singapore 238467

Cambridge University Press is part of Cambridge University Press & Assessment, a department of the University of Cambridge.

We share the University's mission to contribute to society through the pursuit of education, learning and research at the highest international levels of excellence.

www.cambridge.org
Information on this title: www.cambridge.org/9781009484046

DOI: 10.1017/9781108886574

First published 2022
First paperback edition 2024

A catalogue record for this publication is available from the British Library

Library of Congress Cataloging-in-Publication data
Names: Stronks, Martijn, author.
Title: Grasping legal time : temporality and European migration law / Martijn Stronks, Vrije Universiteit, Amsterdam.
Description: Cambridge, United Kingdom ; New York, NY : Cambridge University Press, 2022. | Series: Cambridge asylum and migration studies | Includes bibliographical references and index.
Identifiers: LCCN 2021056194 (print) | LCCN 2021056195 (ebook) | ISBN 9781108835732 (hardcover) | ISBN 9781108886574 (epub)
Subjects: LCSH: Emigration and immigration law–Europe. | Time (Law)–Europe.
Classification: LCC KJC6044 .S77 2022 (print) | LCC KJC6044 (ebook) | DDC 342.408/2–dc23/eng/20220202
LC record available at https://lccn.loc.gov/2021056194
LC ebook record available at https://lccn.loc.gov/2021056195

ISBN 978-1-108-83573-2 Hardback
ISBN 978-1-009-48404-6 Paperback

This book is dedicated to my old friend Pieter Boeles. Our intergenerational friendship is timeless and, alas, ephemeral – like the central theme of this book.

CONTENTS

SERIES EDITOR'S PREFACE

In this novel study, Martijn Stronks shines a light on the ways in which European migration law operates by examining relevant legal processes through the prism of "time." Even as he notes that "[t]ime is allegedly the most widely used noun in the English language," Stronks demands that we critically interrogate this commonplace notion – and specifically that we differentiate between "human time" and "clock time." His contention is that human time is largely overlooked in migration processes, and that this failure to take account of time as lived experience does a real injustice to migrants.

Much of the book is devoted to explicating what the author refers to as "the slithering character of legal time" – which he argues fails to recognize that human time cannot be stopped, that time traveling in actual human time is not possible, and that there is a dissonance between eternal and mortal time. Stronks then makes the case for decentering the place of legal time and giving more attention to human time, noting the countervailing tendency in European law to insist that durable presence in a state's territory gives rise to a claim for inclusion. This, then, is the legal toehold that should allow us to take human time more seriously in the migration realm.

Yet, this book is neither a simple critique of the rigidity of legal time nor an unqualified plea for a refocusing of migration law on human time. Stronks rather seeks to shift our attention to the value in law of the notion of "rootedness," which he sees as embodying an openness to situations not lasting forever and a recognition that there should be a moment in which unlawful presence becomes lawful presence. *Grasping Legal Time* thus allows the reader to imagine a world in which purportedly meritocratic opportunities for inclusion give way to a more fundamentally humane notion of regularization of status.

James C. Hathaway
Editor, Cambridge Asylum and Migration Studies

ACKNOWLEDGMENT

I have worked more than a quarter of my life on the role of time in migration law – that is, to put it in clock time, ten years. I have had numerous conversations with colleagues and friends about this topic, more than I can recall here. This book has been written in the wake of my doctoral research "Grasping Legal Time" that I defended in 2017 at the Vrije Universiteit Amsterdam, and which was supervised by Hemme Battjes, Ger Groot, and Lieneke Slingenberg. I am very indebted to their guidance and comments in that project, which is the fundament on which this book is written.

In this project I have profited from the conversations, insights, support, and sharp and critical comments from Juan Amaya Castro, Jelle van Baardewijk, Hemme Battjes, Pieter Boeles, Elizabeth Cohen, Pieter van der Kolk, Nanda Oudejans, Marcelle Reneman, Lieneke Slingenberg, Karel Smouter, Thomas Spijkerboer, Wouter Veraart, Janna Wessels, and Kartica van der Zon. Thanks to Thomas Spijkerboer for putting me on the track of the relationship between time and vanitas paintings, and for my mother, Anne Marijke Spijkerboer, for teaching me the theological meaning of this art tradition. I am grateful to Jelle van Baardewijk, who came up with the title *Grasping Legal Time*, and directed me – in Heideggerian spirit – to the double meaning of the word grasping. The passages in this book on waiting time are based on the research that I have conducted together with Marcelle Reneman, and which has been published in *Time & Society*. Thanks goes also to students of the Master's Program International Migration and Refugee Law at the Vrije Universiteit Amsterdam for their comments when I presented the argument in this book, and for students of the course Capita Selecta Migratierecht who took the time to scrutinize my dissertation and provide it with valuable comments. Also the students of the Vrije Universiteit Amsterdam Migration Law Clinic deserve my gratitude. Together we wrote the two expert opinions in the cases before the European Court of Justice of the EU (CJEU) of the Ghanaian mother and Eritrean girl that served as introductions to the first two chapters of this book. Thanks to Fadi Fahad for his help in compiling the index. Frances Gilligan and Abigail Neale have been so kind to correct the English, all remaining errors in the text are mine. Many thanks to the team of Cambridge University Press and, in particular, Marianne Nield, Finola O'Sullivan, and Jane Bowbrick, it was a pleasure to work with them.

I further explicitly want to thank Galina Cornelisse whose analytical rigour and perseverance combined with her seemingly endless energy has been a stimulating example and great support in writing and finalizing the book.

Thanks to Kartica van der Zon for the endless conversations we had about the topic of this book, for her enduring support and for the time we share.

This book is dedicated to my oldest friend – in the meaning of age, not the duration of our friendship – Pieter Boeles. Pieter guided me when I took my first steps in the field of migration law more than a decade ago. His influence on the professionalization of Dutch migration law as advocate as well as professor of immigration law at the University of Leiden, and his incessant commitment to the understanding and development of European migration law in the Netherlands can hardly be overstated. His rigorous and original analysis of European and Dutch migration law combined with his glistening writing style have been a great inspiration to me. Pieter – who is almost forty years older than me – showed me that intergenerational friendship is possible; timeless, and ephemeral.

TABLE OF CASES

ICJ

ICJ April 6, 1955, Nottebohm, ICJ Reports 1955

CJEU

CJEU October 27, 1977, Bouchereau, C-30-77
CJEU July 7, 1992, Surinder Singh, C-370/90
CJEU April 29, 2004, Orfanopoulos and Oliveri, C-482/01 and C-493/01
CJEU June 27, 2006, Parliament *v.* Council, C-540/03
CJEU December 11, 2007, Eind, C-291/05
CJEU March 8, 2011, Ruiz Zambrano, C-34/09
CJEU October 18, 2012, Mangat Singh, C-502/10
CJEU November 8, 2012, Iida, C-40/11
CJEU January 31, 2013, H. I. D. and B. A. *v.* Refugee Applications Commissioner and others, C-175/11
CJEU March 12, 2014, O & B, C-456-12
CJEU July 17, 2014, Tahir, C-469/13
CJEU May 10, 2017, Chavez-Vilchez, C-133/15
CJEU April 12, 2018, A & S, C-550/16
CJEU April 17, 2018, Vomero, C-424/16 and C-316/16
CJEU May 2, 2018, K. *v.* the Netherlands and H. F. *v.* Belgium, C-331/16 and C-366/16
CJEU (pending), E. K. *v.* the Netherlands, C-624/20

ECHR

ECHR May 28, 1985, Abdulaziz, Cabalis, and Balkandali *v.* the United Kingdom, 9214/80, 9473/81, and 9474/81
ECHR February 19, 1998, Dahlia *v.* France, 154/1996/773/974
ECHR June 22, 1999, Ajayi *v.* the United Kingdom, 27663/95
ECHR November 2, 2001, Boultif *v.* Switzerland, 54273/00
ECHR October 9, 2003, Slivenko *v.* Austria, 48321/99
ECHR October 18, 2006, Üner *v.* the Netherlands, 46410/99
EHRM April 26, 2007, Konstantinov *v.* the Netherlands, 16351/03
ECHR April 8, 2008, Nnyanzi *v.* the United Kingdom, 21878/08
ECHR June 23, 2008, Maslov *v.* Austria, 1638/03

ECHR January 8, 2009, Joseph Grant *v.* the United Kingdom, 10606/07
ECHR February 17, 2009, Onur *v.* the United Kingdom, 27319/07
ECHR November 24, 2009, Omojudi *v.* the United Kingdom, 1820/08
ECHR January 12, 2010, A. W. Khan, 47486/06
ECHR September 23, 2010, Bousarra *v.* France, 25672/07
ECHR December 9, 2010, Gezginci *v.* Switzerland, 16372/05
ECHR June 14, 2011, Osman *v.* Denmark, 38058/09
ECHR June 28, 2011, Nunez *v.* Norway, 55597/09
ECHR September 20, 2011, A. A. *v.* the United Kingdom, 8000/08
ECHR December 20, 2011, A. H. Khan *v.* the United Kingdom, 6222/10
ECHR February 14, 2012, Antwi *v.* Norway, 26940/10
ECHR December 4, 2012, Butt *v.* Norway, 47017/09
ECHR December 13, 2012, De Souza Ribeiro *v.* France, 22689/07
ECHR April 16, 2013, Udeh *v.* Switzerland, 12020/09
ECHR July 9, 2013, Vinter and others *v.* the United Kingdom, 66069/09, 130/10, and 3896/10
ECHR July 10, 2014, Senigo Longue et Autres c France, 19113/09
EHRM June 30, 2015, A. S. *v.* Switzerland, 39350/13
ECHR May 19, 2016, J. N. *v.* the United Kingdom, 37289/12
ECHR December 13, 2016, Paposhvili *v.* Belgium, 41738/10
ECHR September 14, 2017, Ndidi *v.* the United Kingdom, 41215/14
EHRM July 28, 2020, Pormess *v.* the Netherlands, 25402/14
ECHR July 9, 2021, M. A. *v.* Denmark, 6697/18

TABLE OF TREATIES AND DIRECTIVES

- Treaty for the Functioning of the European Union (TFEU)
- European Convention on Human Rights (ECHR)
- Council Directive 2001/55/EC of July 20, 2001 on minimum standards for giving temporary protection in the event of a mass influx of displaced persons and on measures promoting a balance of efforts between Member States in receiving such persons and bearing the consequences thereof
- Council Directive 2003/86 of September 22, 2003 on the right to family reunification
- Council Directive 2003/109 of November 25, 2003 concerning the status of third-country nationals who are long-term residents
- Council Directive 2004/38/EC of the European Parliament and of the Council of April 29, 2004 on the right of citizens of the Union and their family members to move and reside freely within the territory of the Member States amending Regulation (EEC) No 1612/68 and repealing Directives 64/221/EEC, 68/360/EEC, 72/194/EEC, 73/148/EEC, 75/34/EEC, 75/35/EEC, 90/364/EEC, 90/365/EEC, and 93/96/EEC
- Council Directive 2008/115/EC of the European Parliament and of the Council of December 16, 2008 on common standards and procedures in Member States for returning illegally staying third-country nationals
- Council Directive 2013/32 of June 26, 2013 on common procedures for granting and withdrawing international protection (recast)
- European Parliament and Council Proposal of September 23, 2020 for a Regulation addressing situations of crisis and force majeure in the field of migration and asylum, 2020/0277 (COD)
- The Dutch "Wortelingswet" [literally translated Rootedness Act], *Kamerstukken II* 33068, nr. 1

Introduction

Grasping Legal Time

> To everything there is a season,
> and a time for every purpose under heaven.
>
> Ecclesiastes 3

At the start of this millennium, a Ghanaian woman moved to the Netherlands to live with her Dutch partner. In 2002, her son is born out of wedlock and, because of the Dutch nationality of the father, the child becomes a Dutch national. The mother, however, resides on a residence permit with her family, a residence that is dependent on the relationship with her partner. When this relationship comes to an end in 2006 and the partner subsequently leaves the Netherlands, her residence status is withdrawn. The mother continues to live with her son in the Netherlands, unlawfully but without this being noticed by the Dutch authorities.

In 2012, she successfully applies for a residence permit on the basis of a new ruling of the European Court of Justice of the European Union (CJEU) that allows her to reside with her son on the basis of Article 20 of the Treaty for the Functioning of the European Union (EU). This Zambrano ruling dictates that the mother should be granted a residence status to reside with her son, which she receives in 2013. The reasoning of the CJEU is that if the mother would be sent back to Ghana, the boy's rights as an EU citizen would be impaired because he would effectively been forced to leave the territory of the union to join his mother.[1] In other words, her residence is derivative on the son's union citizenship, which would be harmed if he was to follow the mother to her country of origin.

The new status allows the mother to reside happily out of harm's way for the subsequent five years. At this time, she decides to perpetuate her residence in the Netherlands with an application for permanent residence on the basis of the Long-Term Residence Directive. Alas, this application is declined by the Dutch government, which argues that the specific "Zambrano-residence permit," on the basis of which she has been residing in the country, is by its very nature temporary because the boy will inevitably reach the age of majority and his adulthood will break the relationship of dependency. After all, the residence of the mother is based on the relationship with her child. As a consequence, the mother can no longer derive a residence right based on the EU citizenship of her son when he turns eighteen. Therefore, the mother, who has at that time effectively resided in the Netherlands

[1] CJEU March 8, 2011, *Ruiz Zambrano*, C-34/09, this residence permit is nowadays referred to as the Chavez-Vilchez permit, as a result of a more recent judgment, CJEU May 10, 2017, *Chavez-Vilchez*, C-133/15. See further, H. Kroeze and P. van Elsuwege, "Revisiting Ruiz Zambrano: A Never Ending Story?," *European Journal of Migration and Law* 23, no. 1 (2021).

for more than eighteen years, legally speaking still remains "temporary" within the country. This raises the question of how long can long-term residence legally still be qualified as "temporary"?

This question led to preliminary questions before the CJEU, questions that at the time of writing are still pending.[2] Nevertheless, the case can, already before the CJEU has come to a decision, serve as paradigmatic example for the Janus face of time in migration law. The legal reasoning of the Dutch government shows that the qualification of temporariness of residence is an effective means to differentiate residence entitlements. The mere qualification of the residence as "temporary" is enough to exclude the women from stronger residence entitlements and such is apparently still possible if the migrant has resided up to eighteen years in the country. In other words, time serves as an excellent means to regulate the presence of migrants within a given territory.

The case therefore serves first of all to exemplify the functioning of what Melanie Griffiths has called "temporal governance."[3] I argue in this book that time is indeed one of the most important means for legal control of migrants present within a territory. While migration has become increasingly selective – with smooth migration for some, and difficult or impossible migration for others – time has become more significant for the selection and supervision of migrants. The use of time is not restricted to the qualification of temporariness, in fact it is omnipresent in law,[4] not just in migration law.[5] It is by means of time that migration law makes crucial distinctions between different categories of people, distinctions that have profound consequences for migrants' residence entitlements. As we have seen, some migrants are only allowed to stay temporarily, whilst others may extend their

2 CJEU (pending), *E. K.*, C-624/20.

3 M. B. E. Griffiths, "The Changing Politics of Time in the UK Immigration System," in *Timespace and International Migration*, eds. E. Mavroudi, A. Christou, and B. Page (Camberley: Edward Elgar Publishing, 2017).

4 There is a growing body of literature on the role of time in law, see for an example T. Chowdhury, *Time, Temporality and Legal Judgment* (Abingdon: Taylor & Francis Group, 2020); L. Corrias and L. Francot, eds., *Temporal Boundaries of Law: Time Out of Joint* (London: Routledge, 2018); S. Ranchordás and Y. Roznai, eds., *Time, Law and Change: An Interdisciplinary Study* (London: Hart Publishers, 2020). Not to forget the seminal work of F. Ost, *Le Temps du Droit* (Paris: Editions Odile Jacob, 1999).

5 Also, there is ample literature on the relationship between time and migration, see for an overview B. Anderson, M. Griffiths, and A. Rogers, "Migration, Time and Temporalities: Review and Prospect," Compass Research Resources Paper, 2013. See for a more recent work on time and migration C. Brux, P. K. Hilden, and A. L. O. Middelthon, "'Klokka Tikker, Tiden Gar': Time and Irregular Migration," *Time and Society* 28, no. 4 (2019); T. G. Eule et al., *Migrants before the Law* (Cham: Palgrave, 2019); C. M. Jacobsen, M.-A. Karlsen, and S. Khosravi, eds., *Waiting and the Temporalities of Irregular Migration* (London: Routledge, 2020); S. Robertson, "Time and Temporary Migration: The Case of Temporary Graduate Workers and Working Holiday Makers in Australia," *Journal of Ethnic and Migration Studies* 40, no. 12 (2014), and the references therein. As regards time and migration law, see for example C. Dauvergne and S. Marsden, "The Ideology of Temporary Labour Migration in the Post-global Era," *Citizenship Studies* 18, no. 2 (2014); M. Ineli-Ciger, *Temporary Protection in Law and Practice*, International Refugee Law Series (Leiden: Martinus Nijhoff, 2018); S. Mantu, "Concepts of Time and European Citizenship," *European Journal of Migration and Law* 15, no. 4 (2013); A. Somek, "Solidarity Decomposed: Being and Time in European Citizenship," *University of Iowa Legal Studies Research Paper* nos. 7–13 (2007). The argument in this book does not serve to provide an overview of all of the different forms of time that are at work in migration law, rather the aim is to show the complex relationship one particular form of time, human time, has with the dominant clock time, while both are at work in legal time.

residence or even become nationals. Yet, time can also be used to stipulate whether and how long someone may lawfully stay on the territory; when someone can ask for a renewal of their entitlement or a stronger residence status; while it can equally be used to determine the maximum time of the migration procedure, or the time one has to wait before such a procedure starts. In addition, time can be used to determine whether people can lose their residence entitlements – for example, after committing a criminal offense. In the case of irregular migration, the time human beings have spent on the territory can legally speaking simply be ignored, and prevent migrants from ever being included even though they might claim to have been integrated or "rooted" in the country in the meantime. In other words, it seems as if the possibilities to use time in the legal control of migration are not only numerous but, more strikingly, seemingly limitless. Such temporal governance of the presence of migrants move, as Anderson and Shachar have observed, the border ineluctably inward.[6]

Yet, close scrutiny of the role of time as a means of control also reveals that hidden in the use of time in migration law is an argument for inclusion of migrants based on time. One of the central aims of this book is to make this argument explicit, thereby revealing both pros and cons of the temporal legal control of migrants. And the case of the Ghanaian woman is a great example to use for this argument. While we can read the case as an excellent example of temporal governance, the case could also be understood as precisely how such temporal qualification reaches its limits (and it would not surprise me if the CJEU would come to that conclusion in this case). Calling residence of almost two decades still "temporary" after all begs the question: What is the meaning of such temporariness and can states, normatively and legally, leave migrants endlessly in such a situation of legal limbo? In this book, I argue that temporal governance, such as in this case, finds it limitation in the normative value of human time.

In order to make this normative limitation explicit in this book, I have to simplify the meaning and use of time in law. Hence, I will focus on the role of time in law from different artificial angles. I think it is important to mention this to make clear that the aim of this book is by no means to discuss the role of time in law, or even migration law, from all angles in order to reveal all of the different meanings of time in law. I focus on two conceptions of time in law: human time and clock time. Yet, even the discussion of these conceptions of time risks becoming artificial because clock time and human time are entangled in several ways, so any discussion of their role risks becoming superficial. Still, my aim in this book is not only to show their intricate relationship in the functioning of temporal governance but also to show their fundamental difference. The point of temporal governance is that it is precisely the interplay between the lapse of human time and clock time that enables the legal differentiation based on time. In the end, however, both conceptions of time belong to an entirely different framework, and one of the main conclusions of this book is that legal time can never fully grasp human time. I claim that the eighteen years that the woman has lived in the Netherlands have normative value, irrespective of how they are legally qualified.

[6] B. Anderson, "And About Time Too ... Migration Documentation, and Temporalities," in *Global Insecurities. Paper Trails: Migrants, Documents, and Legal Insecurity* eds. S. B. Horton and J. Heyman (Durham, NC: Duke University Press, 2020), p. 56; A. Shachar, *The Shifting Border: Legal Cartographies of Migration and Mobility* (Manchester: Manchester University Press 2020).

What Then Is Time?

The analysis of time in migration law is pivotal to this book, and at the heart of it is the question of the meaning of time. Time is allegedly the most widely used noun in the English language.[7] Just as in everyday communication, the references to it in migration law are numerous: the time limit for an application, appeal, or a judicial decision; temporary residence permits; long-term residence status; the length of an entry ban; the (adaptable) age of a migrant; the formative years of a child; the right moment to bring forward a legal argument; the time the government has not effectuated a return decision; the review of detention at reasonable intervals of time; a limited period of detention; the traumatic past of a refugee; the future of a migrant worker in the territory; the time since a crime has been committed; the actual risk and so on. In her study *Timewatch: The Social Analysis of Time*, Barbara Adam stresses that in our normal usage of time, we constantly shift between different senses of time and know them intimately without giving much thought to their differences. In her book she wants "to disrupt this natural attitude by giving some attention to those differences and extracting from them clusters of characteristics that allow us to *see* the complexity."[8]

Adam has put forward that one can find a "when time," the time of timing and temporal location of social activities and natural phenomena – for example, when the working day starts, when my daughter was born, when we were young, when Brexit happened, when the Corona measures will be lifted, and so on. Adam stresses that in Western societies, this "when time" is certainly to a large extent based on clocks and calendars, but it is unlikely that they will form the only sources for it. An ordinary working day in the building trade will start just after the sun has risen; a child may be born too early, because the gestation is for a long time; the scheduling of a train may equally be governed by seasonal variations or peak hours, and so on. Moreover, we might think of the past, present, and future through references to events, processes, and social relations. The invention of the art of printing or the declaration of independence but also less historical events such as the moment that someone heard that they were terminally ill can be remembered without knowing the exact date. This leads Adam to conclude that

> [w]e need to recognize that considerations relating to social interactions and the physical environment have not been replaced by the rationalization of time . . . The abstract, quantified, spatialized time of clocks and calendars forms only one aspect of the complexity of meanings associated with the time "when," the time that forms a parameter of our existence and locates us *in* time.[9]

In a similar vein, I try to unravel the meaning of time in migration law. Just as Adam argues that the complexity of meanings associated with time cannot be replaced by the

[7] B. Adam, *Timewatch: The Social Analysis of Time* (Cambridge: Polity Press, 2004), p. 19. She gives a long list of examples in the book, e.g. clock time, winter time, opening times, bad times, the right time for action, the timing of interaction, time of physical processes and social conventions, the time abstract relations of mathematics and concrete relations between people, the lifetime of a person, etc., not to mention all the time-related references such as the minute, the hour, the week, the day, the phase of the moon, the year, Christmas and Easter, productions of growth cycles, generations, etc.

[8] Ibid., p. 20, emphasis in original.

[9] Ibid., p. 21. See also, N. Elias, *An Essay on Time* (Dublin: University College Dublin Press, 2007), pp. 59–60.

rationalized conception of clock time, in law we cannot simply equate time with clock time. So, which sense of time is implied next to the common understanding of the clock and the calendar? Which assumptions inform the *legal time* of migration law? My argument is that the success as well as the shortcoming of the use of time in migration law lies in the difference between legal time and human time. I argue that while time in (migration) law is commonly understood to refer merely to *clock time*, the reference to *human time*, to the temporal experience of the passage of time in human affairs, remains hidden. It is the intricate interplay between clock and human time that is such a perfect means for legal control. However, it is human time that constantly slips through the grasping fingers of legal control. To be sure, this is not to say that such a bifurcation of time is the only meaningful typology of time in law. As Bridget Anderson observes, it is precisely one of the responses to the inability to fully grasp the meaning of time to create different typologies of time that repeatedly put a different aspect of time at the fore.[10] What I endeavor in this book is to show how at the heart of the governance of the presence of migrants within a territory is a sophisticated interplay between human and clock time.

Human Time

Human time can best be characterized in comparison with cosmic time. Time is not purely a human invention; we often call "cosmic time" the time that relates to the seemingly infinite age of the cosmos and its celestial bodies. The latter signifies an endless anonymous time, characterized by motion, measure, and serial order. At least, that is the representation of it in science, where it is constituted merely by relations of simultaneity and succession between abstract "instants" demarcated by "before" and "after."[11] Characteristic for the cosmic perception of time is its impersonal character: it is the time that is not dependent on a human observer,[12] or "at least whose endless passage is above and beyond any one

10 Anderson, "And About Time Too … Migration Documentation, and Temporalities," p. 55. Anderson's typology is closely related to what I argue in this book, yet slightly different. Anderson distinguishes between the bureaucratic time of the state and the subjective time of the individual. Even though I also contrast the usage of time in governance by states with the biological and subjective time of individuals, I additionally show how this individual time of the human being is precisely the locus of the state's temporal governance. In other words, while I argue that temporal governance is limited by the normative quality of human time, at the same time, this human time is intricately entangled with the chronological time of the clock in the exercise of temporal governance. The two are therefore not only opposed but also interwoven.

11 This and the following conceptual demarcation is largely based on M. Muldoon, "Time, Self, and Meaning in the Works of Henri Bergson, Maurice Merleau-Ponty, and Paul Ricoeur," *Philosophy Today* 35, no. 3 (1991), p. 254, see in that Article most notably the first two footnotes for a clear conceptual description. Ricoeur uses many of these concepts as well, albeit not always after clearly defining the differences between them, e.g. P. Ricoeur, *Time and Narrative*. Volume 3 (Chicago: The University of Chicago Press, 1988); P. Ricoeur, *Memory, History, Forgetting* (Chicago: The University of Chicago Press, 2004). See for a very readable introduction to this "cosmic time," S. Hawking, *A Brief History of Time* (New York: Bantam books, 1995).

12 That is to say, as Bergson remarks, without an elementary memory that unities two instants as the former preceding the latter, there would be no instant, no succession and no time, reference taken from Muldoon, "Time, Self, and Meaning in the Works of Henri Bergson, Maurice Merleau-Ponty, and Paul Ricoeur," original reference from H. Bergson, *Durée et Simultanitéité* (Paris: Alcan, 1923), p. 61.

person's ability to generate or destroy," as Mark Muldoon has put it succinctly.[13] It is the form of time that would also exist without the presence of human beings (at least that is what we assume). Or, in the words of Bridget Anderson while referring to what she calls natural time (including both biological and astronomical times):

> I mean temporal passing that proceeds irrespective of interference by humans: the length of daylight, the seasons, processes of aging, and so on. It is not that this time cannot be bypassed – heavy blinds can shut out daylight, heating can mimic summer, cosmetic surgery alleviates the physical signs of aging – but there is a process that proceeds nonetheless, or is ready to take over as soon as interventions ceases.[14]

A large part of my argument in this book is meant to show how three characteristic aspects of human time are easily overlooked in the legal management of the presence of migrants. These characteristics come to the fore when comparing the time of the cosmos. The latter is to be distinguished from human time in the first place because human beings are mortal, which means that their time necessarily punctuates the (seemingly) endless cosmic time. This also implies that the time of human beings is, as mentioned earlier, irreversible, and moreover that it cannot be stopped. Human time is, secondly, always the time of someone and this lived experience is therefore not reducible to the mere passage of cosmic time. Thirdly, human time is characterized by temporality: the need for a temporal present, which implies a past and a future.

Such a temporal present is elementary for human time and is related to the other two characteristics. As Muldoon rightly puts forward, the temporal present is "always the product of some principle of unity in the midst of change that draws upon the operation of perception, discrimination, memory and anticipation."[15] The present constitutes a unity that in mere anonymous cosmic time does not exist. The very function of such a unifying principle is to mediate precisely between the time of the cosmos on the one hand and the lived experience of a mortal human being on the other hand. In order to further introduce this complicated point, I would like to briefly deliberate the best known and oldest example of such a principal, Augustine's *distentio animi*.

In his *Confessions*, Augustine famously questioned how time could be measured if the present has no extension. After all, the moment slips away time and again.

> [Present time] is measured while it passes, but when it has passed it is not measured; for then there is nothing that could be measured ... Therefore, from what is not yet, through what has no length, it passes into what is now no longer ... But in what "length," then, do we measure passing time? Is it in the future, from which it passes over? But what does not yet exist cannot be measured. Or, is it in the present, through which it passes? But what has no length we cannot measure. Or is it in the past into which it passes? But what is no longer we cannot measure.[16]

[13] Muldoon, "Time, Self, and Meaning in the Works of Henri Bergson, Maurice Merleau-Ponty, and Paul Ricoeur," p. 254.

[14] Anderson, "And About Time Too ... Migration Documentation, and Temporalities," pp. 55–6.

[15] In the course of this book, I will discuss one of these unifying principles: durational consciousness of Bergson. Muldoon further puts forward "*distentio animi*" (Augustine), "transcendental ego" (Husserl), "lived body" (Merleau-Ponty), "*Dasein*" (Heidegger), and the commonly used "self." Muldoon, "Time, Self, and Meaning in the Works of Henri Bergson, Maurice Merleau-Ponty, and Paul Ricoeur," p. 254.

[16] Augustine, *Confessions*, trans. A. C. Outler (Grand Rapids, MI: Christian Classics Ethereal Library, 1955), book XI, chapter XXI, par. 27 (or pagenumber 197).

We see here that the anonymous passage of cosmic time does not easily fit the human frame of time as past, present, and future.[17]

Augustine's answer to these persisting ontological questions is that we measure time in the mind (*distentio animi*). In the mind, the future and the past are present by way of expectation and remembrance. It is our attention that has continuity, stresses Augustine, through which what is present may become absent in the past. "Therefore, future time, which is nonexistent, is not long; but 'a long future' is 'a long expectation of the future.' Nor is time past, which is now no longer, long; a 'long past' is 'a long memory of the past.'"[18] Augustine's solution is a rigorous limitation of time to the mere present of the conscious mind.

His thought experiment shows the clear distinction between the seemingly endless passage of cosmic time and the human time of the temporal experience as past, present, and future.[19] In cosmic time, there is no past, present, nor future, for this implies an observer who is situated *in time*. Human time is always the time of someone, who constitutes a present, implying a future and a past, whose time is finite due to their mortality. As we later observe, law takes into account human time, for example, by creating the temporal present of a legal decision but mostly it makes use of yet another form of time.

Clock Time

Before the invention of the mechanical clock, time would be measured on the sun, moon, or stars, or even running water or the sand in a sandglass. Regarding celestial bodies, the measurement would differ along with the slight differences of night and day and seasons. The measurement without reference to the sky, however, would lack the relationship with nature and would only be based on the constant and reliable stream of sand or water.

In contrast with natural rhythms, the time frame of the clock is characterized by invariability, context independence, and precision. It shares these criteria with the measurement of water or the sandglass, while it still refers to natural rhythms. Until approximately 1840, practically every city in the world made use of local time, based on the meridian passage of the sun. The local habits for the measurement of the other hours of the day could differ to a great extent. For example, until the nineteenth century, the Italian day started at sunset, meaning that Italian noon fell around eighteen hours into the day.[20]

Most notably, the electric telegraph and the railways increased the need for a universal standardized time. The speed with which long distances could be traveled made it increasingly problematic to work with all kinds of different local times. The standardized clock time, which was determined in Washington, DC, at the International Meridian Conference

17 McTaggart has referred to this as the problem of the A-series and B-series of time that must both be rejected for inconsistency (and therefore prove the "unreality" of time), see J. E. McTaggart, "The Unreality of Time," *Mind: A Quarterly Review of Psychology and Philosophy* 17 (1908).

18 Augustine, *Confessions*, trans. Outler, book XI, chapter XXVIII, par. 37 (or pagenumber 203).

19 See for a readable, critical, and more elaborate discussion of Augustine's *distentio animi*, P. Ricoeur, *Time and Narrative*. Volume 1 (Chicago: The University of Chicago Press, 1984), chapter 1. Ricoeur puts forward that in resolving the enigma of measurement, Augustine reaches the ultimate characterization of human time. For a clear introduction to more philosophy of temporality, see D. C. Hoy, *The Time of Our Lives: A Critical History of Temporality* (Cambridge, MA: The MIT Press, 2009).

20 K. Lippincott, U. Eco, and E. H. Gombrich, *The Story of Time* (London: Merrell Publishers, 2003).

in 1884, made sure that everywhere on the globe one hour of clock time would have the same duration. The standardized time replaced the variable "hours" that changed with the seasons and the continuum of "local time." This standardized form of time became an omnipresent part of our contemporary lives. One could say that we live in, to borrow a phrase from Robert Hassan, "clock time modernity,"[21] or in times of "chronopolitics."[22]

This standardization of time, however, begs the question: What does clock time refer to, after all? The measure of a clock is designed on the principle of invariance, every time-unit is measured exactly the same time and again, while the "natural time" based on the local rhythms of days and seasons is characterized by fundamental variance. The hours of daylight change minimally every day, the constellation of the stars do not recur in exactly the same position, not every year has 365 days. This was after all the very reason for the introduction of standard time; yet, the result is that it makes the measure of the clock qualitatively different from what it measures.[23]

It is this qualitative difference that differentiates clock time from the time of the cosmos, but also from human time. At least that is what the French philosopher Henri Bergson (1859–1941) argues in his *Time and Free Will*,[24] which was originally published as *Essai sur les données immédiates de la conscience* in 1889. Bergson argues that there is a confusion of concrete duration with abstract clock time. He shows that the idea of a homogeneous and measurable time is an artificial concept based on the intrusion of space into the realm of pure duration. Alongside this homogenous understanding of the time of the clock, Bergson argued that for a proper temporal understanding, a heterogeneous time of duration should be incorporated. Such duration could not be put on a par with standardized clock time, for the latter reduces the lapse of time to a series of moments that succeed each other. Bergson, on the other hand, sought for an understanding of time that is not based on space; thereby taking up the problem of extension where Augustine left it. In Chapter 3, I argue that for a proper understanding of migrants becoming "rooted" ("rootedness" is often used as an argument for inclusion of migrants over time), this lived experience of a finite human time is crucial. It is this form of durational time that cannot be fully grasped by clock time, which is so central to legal control. I expose in Chapter 1 how this homogenous and general character of the clock makes time so appropriate for legal control.

In literature, clock time is often discussed together with calendar time.[25] Whereas clock time and calendar time might often be taken together, they have a different meaning and history. It is important to briefly discuss their difference, for clock and calendar time will both play a role in the analysis of legal time. For reasons of readability, I will just refer to clock time (albeit, often the time of the calendar is at stake, e.g., when time is expressed in terms of days, months, or years). It is their rationalized, homogenous, and general character that allows for objectification and quantification that is important for my analysis of legal time.

[21] See chapter 2 of R. Hassan, *Empires of Speed: Time and the Acceleration of Politics and Society* (The Hague: Brill, 2009).

[22] I. Klinke, "Chronopolitics: A Conceptual Matrix," *Progress in Human Geography* 37, no. 5 (2012).

[23] Adam, *Timewatch*, pp. 24–5.

[24] H. Bergson, *Time and Free Will: An Essay on the Immediate Data of Consciousness* [Essai sur les données immédiates de la conscience], trans. F. L. Pogson (New York: Dover Publications, 2001).

[25] See e.g. J. Postill, "Clock and Calendar Time: A Missing Anthropological Problem," *Time & Society* 11, nos. 2/3 (2002).

Paul Ricoeur argues that calendar time is the first attempt to bridge the gap between what I have called human time and the time of the cosmos. Other mediations that bridge the time of the cosmos with human time (and thereby enable history) are, according to Ricoeur, the "succession of generations" and "archives, documents and traces."[26] The short time span of mortal human beings is situated on a calendar and similarly related to the endless time of the cosmos.

Moreover, the calendar constitutes a socialized form of time, allegedly a necessary condition of the life of societies as well as of individuals in a society. Benedict Anderson famously argues that the calendar plays an important role in the construction of national imaginations. "The idea of a sociological organism moving calendrically through homogenous, empty time is a precise analogue of the idea of the nation, which also is conceived as a solid community moving steadily down (or up) history."[27] The calendrical appearance of newspapers, for example, importantly provides the steady onward clocking of homogenous empty time.

> If Mali disappears from the pages of *The New York Times* after two days of famine reportage, for months on end, readers do not for a moment imagine that Mali has disappeared or that famine has wiped out all its citizens. The novelistic format of the newspaper assures them that somewhere out there the "character" Mali moves along quietly, awaiting its next reappearance in the plot.[28]

The clock and the calendar are state-standardized conceptions of time, and they are both necessary for modern states to function.[29]

Both calendar time and cosmic time are constituted as a uniform, infinite continuum that is segmentable at will, yet our conception of calendar time is interlaced with the temporality of human time. Calendars are constituted by a founding moment (Christ, Buddha, the beginning of the reign of a monarch, etc.) determined by a set of units of measurement, and due to this, it is possible to traverse time in two directions, from the past to the present and from the present toward the past.[30] For this reason, it becomes possible to relate different events, experiences, and lives to each other by reference to a common standard of time.

After all, without the temporal human understanding of time as the present, as the "today," of which there is a "tomorrow" and a "yesterday," we would not be able to make any sense of a new event that breaks with a preceding era, that inaugurates a course of events entirely different from what preceded it. One needs a sense of memory and expectation to be able to *traverse* time, for we need to have a sense of the present moment to be able to discern this from earlier and later moments in time. In this book's analysis, I will clump together clock time and calendar time, just as in ordinary parlance we usually refer to both times together.

[26] Ricoeur, *Time and Narrative*. Volume 3, p. 109. Ricoeur elaborately argues that the relationship between time and history is marked by narrativity. There is therefore a clear overlap between human identity and history, they are firmly entangled.

[27] B. Anderson, *Imagined Communities: Reflections on the Origin and Spread of Nationalism* (London: Verso, 2016), p. 26.

[28] Ibid., p. 33. [29] D. Gross, "Temporality and the Modern State," *Theory and Society* 14, no. 1 (1985).

[30] Ricoeur, *Time and Narrative*. Volume 3, p. 105.

Legal Time and Lawful Time

Carol Greenhouse argues that in Western legal systems, it is law's cultural role to precisely preserve the indeterminacies of time that follow from the distinction between individual lifetimes and the social order.[31] One of the aims of this book is to show how this indeterminacy in legal time is at work; stemming from the intricate relationship between clock time and human time. The strain that I describe in legal time follows from the fact that human time is structurally different from legal time, a problem that cannot be solved in legal time. Yet, it can be acknowledged, and taking into account the peculiar character of human time in itself has normative value. When I refer to legal time in this book, I also refer to the complex and sometimes contradictory usage of time in (migration) law. However, this legal time cannot be equated with lawful time. Lawful time has a very specific meaning in migration law, as it entails the legally permitted presence over time of a migrant on a territory. Its counterpart is unlawful time, which designates the presence in the territory without legal authorization.

The Arrow of Time

This book is about the governance of residence entitlements of migrants present within a certain territory by means of time and the question of the arrow of time is one of the central elements of the argument that I put to the fore. Yet, the meaning of such an arrow of time is far from straightforward, the different significations of time that have already come across equally complicate the question as to whether the process of time has a certain direction.

Clock time is not linear, at least, if we understand it as the mechanical device that shows the time of day. After all, merely on the basis of a clock, one cannot tell what day it is, and on a traditional clock, one could not even tell whether it is day or night. Clock time is, technically speaking, cyclical not linear. Yet, clock time is often clumped together with calendar time, as we observed earlier, and the calendar seems, at least at first sight, to have an arrow; it refers to time moving forward.

Human time equally has a direction, it goes from birth to death, and it cannot be stopped.[32] That is not to say, however, that human time, as I described it earlier, can only be understood as moving in a certain direction. Human time is also determined by temporality, the need for a temporal present, which constitutes a past and a future and such temporality has no direction. As Norbert Elias explains, while concepts like "earlier" and "later" might be related to a sequence that develops in a certain direction (like the calendar), terms like "now," "today," and "past, present, and future" depend on the persons or groups that refer to these positions and therefore do not have a general linear trajectory.[33]

Yet, if we take this into account, the functioning of the calendar also becomes less straightforward. As pointed out earlier, the calendar presupposes human temporality, which allows for the possibility of "time traveling." After all, a calendar does not show

[31] C. J. Greenhouse, "Just in Time: Temporality and the Cultural Legitimation of Law," *Yale Law Journal* 98 (1989), p. 1641.

[32] Cosmic time also has an arrow, which goes in the same direction, see for a helpful introduction to this Hawking, *A Brief History of Time*, pp. 148–9.

[33] Elias, *An Essay on Time*, p. 65

what time it is in abstracto, the calendar presumes the present moment of a spectator, which constitutes the "now," from the past and future to follow. Still, both the calendar and human time can be related to the arrow of time. In both cases, the temporal passing proceeds irrespective of interference by humans, or is beyond anyone's capacity to generate or destroy it, as mentioned earlier. One can act *as if* it is still 2010, such as a relevant moment for the legal decision, we cannot actually turn back time. As we will see, this trait of the calendar – this possibility of time traveling based on the difference between human time and calendar time – is one of the characteristics that makes clock and calendar time apt for temporal governance.

What about the process of migrants being present over a long period of time within a certain territory, does such a process follow a certain direction? Bridget Anderson claims that in research on migration and migration policy one finds an assumption that migrants move from being temporary to permanent and integrated in a linear progress over the course of time.[34] And if one was to have a look at for example the structure and principles of the European Long-Term Residence Directive, one might actually start to believe that migrants generally receive stronger residence entitlements over the course of time because their long-term residence shows that "the person has put down roots in the country."[35] Yet, as Anderson argues, the social reality does not align with the reality that these legal norms might suggest – not only is the process "far from smooth, but many people find themselves in prolonged liminal statuses."[36]

Claiming that the development of certain rights follows a certain clear direction seems to take into account a teleological if not Enlightenment conception of the relationship between rights and progress of time.[37] Such a "chrono-logic of rights," as Bonnie Honig calls it, focuses on the right-as-symbol and not on the actual behavior of a right. "The right-as-symbol is the right as it is seen by those who privilege as its meaning its capacity to be extended and tapped in certain ways that fulfil what they see as its true function or promise, regardless of its operations."[38] In such a perspective, the social reality of people finding themselves in prolonged liminal statuses might be the malfunctioning of the right, it does not contest its intrinsic arrow of time.

A chrono-logic of rights is a tale of law's progress, and does not tell us much about the practice of the right. Such an account of law's temporality also neglects the implicit exclusionary normativity at work in law. Building on the work of Fabian, Johannes Anne McNevin goes as far to argue that such a progressive temporality, such a chrono-logic of rights, even functions as a means of exclusion, or at least as a way to justify the waiting and delays that migrants endure at the borders and in their trajectory toward citizenship.

> In these cases, progressive temporality, including the assumption that the future of citizenship is universally better than its past, is part of what holds in place a recurring

[34] Anderson, "And About Time Too . . . Migration Documentation, and Temporalities," p. 53.

[35] Recital 6, Long-Term Residence Directive (Directive 2003/109).

[36] Anderson, "And About Time Too . . . Migration Documentation, and Temporalities," p. 53.

[37] Ost, *Le Temps du Droit*, p. 179–80. Ost points at three characteristics of such an optimist Enlightment concept of progression: it valorizes the future to be superior to the past; the near future is foreseeable and transparent in a rational and mobilizing discourse; and the future is a progressive actualization of the essence of man, the accomplishment of the promise of humanity (p. 179).

[38] B. Honig, *Emergency Politics: Paradox, Law, Democracy* (Princeton, NJ: Princeton University Press, 2009) p. 55.

> present in which differential access to citizenship is continually reinforced. The sense of a linear temporal trajectory – that one threshold step leads to another in a movement towards citizenship – on one hand tempers discontent with the promise of citizenship-to-come. It also tempers dissent because waiting patiently, in the right way, becomes part of the criteria for citizenship's future acquisition.[39]

The promise of citizenship as a way to legitimize delays and waiting might indeed in certain instances of waiting be an important element of the techniques of inclusion and exclusion, just as "integration schemes" have been criticized for legitimizing legal and symbolic precarity for admitted migrants more than fostering the integration of newcomers in the host country.[40] At the same time, for certain migrants, the promise of citizenship will be fulfilled, migrants do receive long-term resident status or successfully naturalize. That might be precisely the way to temper discontent with the promise of citizenship-to-come for others, it is *also* the fulfillment of that promise to some.

Yet, it is clear that such a promise is not a function of a mere lapse of time. Still, one of the central aims in this book is precisely to argue that residence entitlements of migrants *should* be linked to the amount of time that they have spent in the territory. The arrow of time, which I distinguish in the governance of the presence of migrants, is therefore not one of empirical fact, nor a function of clock time. Contemporary European migration law increasingly provides evidence to the contrary; especially regarding the treatment of asylum seekers and irregular migrants, there seems to be almost no relationship between lapse of time and the possibilities to end their situation of "stuckedness."[41] However, the normative argument that I put to the fore is not linked to lapse of clock time but to the progress of human time and finds its value in the latter's finite, irreversible, and unstoppable character. I claim that there is – or should be – a normative arrow of time at work in the regulation of the presence of migrants within a given territory.

The Argument

The argument in this book consists of three interrelated discussions of the connections between clock time, human time, and legal control. The basis of my analysis is a discussion of how time is used in migration law. The focus will be on how legal time is central to controlling the presence of migrants on a territory and start by endeavoring to unravel the intricate interplay between clock and human time in legal time.

It is the objective and calculable character of clock time that makes it so suited to the manipulation of rules. For example, a term for naturalization of five years can easily be changed to seven years, precisely because of its objective, calculable, and formal character. A formal time criterion is easier to use than, for example, material integration tests that require a complex and individual assessment on a case-by-case basis. Moreover, one of the

39 A. McNevin, "Time and the Figure of the Citizen," *International Journal of Politics, Culture, and Society* 33 (2020), p. 550.

40 T. M. de Waal, "Conditional Belonging: Evaluating Integration Requirements from a Social Equality Perspective," *Journal of Intercultural Studies* 41, no. 2 (2020).

41 A. M. Reneman and M. C. Stronks, "What Are They Waiting For? The Use of Acceleration and Deceleration in Asylum Procedures by the Dutch Government," *Time & Society* 30, no. 3 (2021); M. Tazzioli, "The Temporal Borders of Asylum: Temporality of Control in the EU Border Regime," *Political Geography* 64, no. 15 (2018).

advantages of clock time criteria is, as Elizabeth Cohen has argued, that they refer to processes that happen in time but that would otherwise be hard to put into words, let alone in clear material criteria.[42] The relationship between time spent on the territory, rootedness, and integration exactly serves to prove this point. After all, processes of integration and rootedness clearly happen in time but at a different pace and with diverse outcomes for everyone. A simple time criterion is useful because it relates to such processes, without becoming too arbitrary or too individualistic. Time enables quantification, and this allows for a fairly easy and general application of the rule to individual cases.

Nonetheless, it is not just clock time that is being used in migration law. The object of governance in migration law is after all the life of the migrant, and this is characterized by human time, the time of someone, which constitutes a past, present, and future, can just as well be the object of temporal control. Most notably, categorizing legal presence within a territory as "temporary" is a way that the prospected or assigned future of the migrant is used to make important legal differentiations. Yet, simultaneously in the use of deadlines or the qualification of time spent within the territory, the object is the actual human time of someone. I argue in Chapter 1 that the interplay between clock and human time makes legal time particularly apt for "temporal governance," for the control of the presence of migrants by means of time.

That said, the interactions between human and clock time in legal time can also be strained; in the end, the two conceptions of time are fundamentally different. The second discussion in this book focuses on the difference between human time and legal time. After having argued how clock time is apt for legal control, the complex relations between human time and legal time will be central. The limit to the manipulability of legal time lies in the fact that legal time can never fully grasp human time. Whereas human time has an important role to play in law, it is also a source for constant problems. In the second chapter, two philosophical problems of time are discussed: the problem of extension; and the problem of eternity.

Based on the work of the French philosopher Henri Bergson, I argue that the problem of extension, or the problem of lapse of time, is at the heart of the usage of time in law. Clock time might be very suitable because it can refer to processes that would otherwise be very difficult to grasp, but the problem is that with the measurement of the clock, the durable presence of migrants within a territory can never be fully captured. Clock time presumes a form of exteriority that fixates time in the moment, from which other moments can be discerned and a line can be drawn. Yet, the opposite of such an exterior perspective of time does not freeze time in the moment but its succession can hardly be grasped in any comprehensive analysis. This leads to what I call the formal/material time problem, the problem that if one uses a formal clock time criterion, one loses reference to the individual process (of rootedness or integration), whereas if one uses a material criterion, eventually the reference to lapse of time is lost. Obviously, in contemporary migration law both criteria are used often simultaneously, for example, naturalization criteria often complements a probationary period of time with an integration test. Still, the point here is rather that the durable human time of a migrant within a territory always risks escaping the grasp of legal time.

[42] E. F. Cohen, *The Political Value of Time* (Cambridge: Cambridge University Press, 2018).

The second substantial discussion in this chapter is based on the work of the German philosopher Martin Heidegger. Heidegger criticizes clock time for secretly making use of an eternal conception of time: time as a moving image of eternity, which is always present and endless. This conception of time is fundamentally different from human time, which is characterized by its finite character. Human time is singular, finite, can be neither stopped nor traversed because it is characterized by mortality. Whilst one of the advantages of legal time is that it is general, endless, can be paused, and traversed in both directions, these characteristics are all at odds with human time. I elucidate that in legal time this can lead to frictions, or at the very least, simply forgetting the character and value of human time is unjust. I hold that human time has value, simply because of its peculiar characteristics: it is a scarce good, human time is finite, cannot be stopped nor traversed. That modest observation – that human time has a direction and is finite and is therefore in the end profoundly different from legal time – is the shortest version of the conclusion of this book.

The aim of this book is precisely that – to bring to the forefront the character and value of human time in the usage of legal time in migration law. I argue in the third chapter that hidden in plain sight, as Elizabeth Cohen nicely puts it, is a temporal argument for the inclusion of migrants who reside long term within the territory based on their human time. In short, human time within a territory matters. I will use the term jus temporis to refer to this argument, following Elizabeth Cohen who has coined this concept.[43] I argue that jus temporis in fact is at work in contemporary (European) migration law, and that it functions alongside arguments for inclusion that are also based on presence within a territory, such as jus domicilii and jus nexi. At the heart of the argument of jus temporis is "rootedness" as grounds for inclusion, a concept that I propose should be distinguished from "integration." In literature, case-law, and statutes, these terms are often used interchangeably: frequently as arguments for inclusion of migrants over time, yet without precisely pinpointing their (respective) meaning(s). I argue that integration has a normative and meritocratic meaning: it relates to the ascribed values and norms of a particular society; certain knowledge of the language; and qualifies the behavior and character of someone's presence within a territory. Rootedness, however, has a more factual character, it simply refers to the lapse of human time and gives it value because it is finite, irreversible, and cannot be stopped. Both are at work in migration law, I hold.

For that reason, I argue that one can discern in legislation and case-law another principle that works alongside normative, material time criteria, albeit silently and often confused or equated with integration: becoming rooted or rootedness. References to rootedness can be found in EU law, such as the Long-term Resident Directive, case-law on Article 8 ECHR (European Convention on Human Rights), and in national debates about the regularization of irregular migrants.[44] Rootedness is in fact omnipresent in contemporary migration law, although it is often implicitly at work. Even though most countries in Europe use integration criteria for residence entitlements and naturalization, such countries almost without

[43] E. F. Cohen, "Citizenship and the Law of Time in the United States," *Duke Journal of Constitutional law & Public Policy* 53, no. 8 (2013) .

[44] See recital 12, Long-Term Residence Directive (Directive 2003/109); ECHR October 18, 2006, *Üner* v. *the Netherlands*, 46410/99, paragraph 58; and e.g. the Dutch "Wortelingswet" [literally translated Rootedness Act], *Kamerstukken II* 33068, nr. 1.

exception also require individuals to spend formal time on the territory before applying for such entitlements.[45]

I argue that rootedness should be defined as the entanglement of presence within a territory with the lapse of finite and irreversible human time of someone's life. That might sound more cryptic than it is; what I simply mean is that the lapse of human time has normative value, and that human time should not be wasted. No matter whether the time that a migrant has spent within a territory has been qualified as positive or negative, by oneself, others or the (imagined) communities, the time has value as human time. Rootedness should therefore not be confused with inclusion, acceptation, assimilation, or integration. Rootedness is merely the reference to someone's human time within a territory.

From the outset, it is important to note that I do not intend to argue that this ius temporis should replace existing grounds for inclusion, such as ius soli, ius sanguinis, ius nexi, or ius domicilii. My argument is closely related to the arguments for inclusion after birth, ius nexi and ius domicilii, and to a large extent coincides with the latter. I do think, however, that it is important to make a distinguishing claim based on time, because in any claim for inclusion, time plays an important but implicit role. Time, ties, and domicile are often clumped together in claims for inclusion as if they do not have a different argumentative force. I aim to show that all three have their own merits but that the temporal argument can be valued as a separate ground for inclusion, together with ties and domicile.

The temporal argument consists of two elements central to this book: human time structurally escapes legal time, and rootedness is a temporal ground for inclusion. Since human time can never be fully grasped by law, any attempt to find a criterion that does give full justice to the presence of migrants on the territory over time is doomed to fail. Nevertheless, this is not a recipe for skepticism or the lack of legal criteria – quite the contrary. My conclusion in this book is that an ius temporis should (and in fact often does) always consist of the following two elements: the *possibility* to gain (stronger) residence entitlements in the future, and eventually the *impossibility* to remove the person from the territory.

45 An interesting and still rather limited exception to this rule is the application for citizenship on the basis of money. In some European countries, there is the possibility to invest a very large sum of money in the economy of the country, which then serves as ground for naturalization (without the prerequisite of spending time on the territory beforehand), see also A. Shachar, "Citizenship for Sale?," in *The Oxford Handbook of Citizenship*, eds. A. Shachar et al. (Oxford: Oxford University Press, 2017), pp. 789–816.

1

The Virtues of Legal Time

> Waiting is one of the privileged ways of experiencing the effect of power, and the link between time and power – and one would need to catalogue, and analyse, all the behaviours associated with the exercise of power over other people's time both on the side of the powerful (adjourning, deferring, delaying, raising false hopes, or, conversely, rushing, taking by surprise) and on the side of the "patient" as they say in the medical universe, one of the sites par excellence of anxious, powerless waiting.
>
> Pierre Bourdieu, *Pascalian Meditations*, 2000 AD

> Have you never noticed that when a Russian says "four hours" it means no more to him than "one hour" does to us? The idea comes easily to mind that the nonchalance with which these people treat time has something to do with the savage expanse of their land. Too much room – too much time. It has been said that they are a nation with time on their hands – they can afford to wait. We Europeans can't wait. We have just as little time as our noble, tidily segmented continent has space; we must carefully husband the resources of the former just as we do those of the latter – put time and space to use, good use, engineer!
>
> Thomas Mann, *Magic Mountain*, 1924 AD

This chapter commences with the story of a girl at a young age, with which characterization we find ourselves *in medias res.* On February 26, 2014, an Eritrean teenager applied for asylum in the Netherlands. After a rather quick asylum procedure, her claim was successful and she received a residence permit on October 21, 2014. The permit was valid for five years, with effect from the moment that her application was submitted. Like all refugees, the girl had the right to family reunification, so immediately after she was granted refugee status, she requested to be reunited with her parents. The procedure for family reunification of refugees is, according to the European Union (EU) Family Reunification Directive (Directive 2003/86), more favorable than general regulations for family reunification. The reason for this is that the refugees' flight from their country prevents them from leading a normal family life there. Specifically, this means children can be reunited with their family members, including their parents, without further restrictions (such as integration tests or income requirements). Adults can reunite with their parents but only if the parents are dependent on them and lack family support in their country of origin. Although both rules are more favorable than the rules for nonrefugee cases of family reunification, it made quite a difference whether the Eritrean girl was a minor or an adult. In the former case, her parents could reunite with her, in the latter, only if her parents were dependent on her and lacked family support in Eritrea. So, the pivotal question to this case of family reunification was: How old is the girl?

As plain and simple as this question might seem at first, it led to a fierce legal dispute. For the issue was that between the time when the girl requested asylum and the moment that she received refugee protection, she had attained legal majority. On June 2, 2014, she became eighteen years old. Due to a lapse of time in the procedure, however short, the facts changed drastically, entailing far-reaching consequences for the girl. In her case, as an adult, the girl would have no opportunity to reunite with her parents since they were not dependent on her. But as a child, she would have an unrestricted right to reunite with her parents. So how old was the girl?

The Dutch government argued that the relevant moment to establish the age of the girl was the moment of the decision to grant her refugee status (eighteen). The girl argued that the relevant moment should be the moment of her entry into the Netherlands and her asylum application (seventeen). Proceedings went all the way to the Dutch Council of State, the highest administrative judge in migration law, which, in its turn, raised a preliminary question with the European Court of Justice of the EU (CJEU).[1] On April 12, 2018, roughly two months before the Eritrean girl turned twenty-two, the CJEU declared that the girl was, legally speaking, seventeen years old, and could therefore reunite with her parents.

The case of the Eritrean girl serves as an example of "temporal governance," a term coined by Melanie Griffiths to refer to the diverse manifestations of the role of time in governing migration.[2] Temporal governance can be seen as a governmental strategy to discipline and control migrants by means of time. Indeed, power operates as much through temporal devices as it does through spatial control.[3] As Griffiths shows, migration is not an exception to the central use of time in the operationalization of state power. This politics of time, in some fields called chronopolitics,[4] plays a pivotal role in the governance of migration and borders.[5] There is a growing body of anthropological literature on the different and contradictory forms of time at work in migrant experiences. Time can be stagnated, such as is clearly the case in waiting times in asylum centers or camps,[6] but it can also be "frenzied," with sudden ruptures and accelerations.[7] Moreover, Martina Tazzioli argues that frequently changing the temporal deadlines for procedures of entry at the borders of Europe, "is part of a mode of government through confusion and uncertainty that in itself produces effects of temporal suspension and spatial confinement on

1 CJEU April 12, 2018, *A & S*, C-550/16, the Migration Law Clinic of the Amsterdam Centre for Migration and Refugee Law wrote an expert opinion in this case, which I supervised together with Lieneke Slingenberg, see www.migrationlawclinic.org/2018/04/12/cjeu-date-asylum-application-decisive-for-right-to-family-reunification-unaccompanied-minor/.

2 Griffiths, "The Changing Politics of Time in the UK Immigration System."

3 Eule et al., *Migrants before the Law*, p 149.

4 Klinke, "Chronopolitics."

5 S. B. Cwerner, "The Times of Migration," *Journal of Ethnic and Migration Studies* 27, no. 1 (2001).

6 R. Anderson, "Time and the Migrant Other: European Border Controls and the Temporal Economics of Illegality," *American Anthropologist* 116, no. 4 (2014); M. B. E. Griffiths, "Frenzied, Decelerating and Suspended: the Temporal Uncertainties of Failed Asylum Seekers and Immigration Detainees," *Compas Research Resources Papers*, no. 105 (2013); M. B. E. Griffiths, "Out of Time: The Temporal Uncertainties of Refused Asylum Seekers and Immigration Detainees," *Journal of Ethnic and Migration Studies* 40, no. 12 (2014); S. Khosravi, "Waiting," in *A COMPAS Anthology*, eds. B. Anderson and M. Keith (Oxford: COMPAS, 2014), p. 74.

7 Griffiths, "Frenzied, Decelerating and Suspended"; Griffiths, "The Changing Politics of Time in the UK Immigration System"; M. B. E. Griffiths, "Living with Uncertainty: Indefinite Immigration Detention," *Journal of Legal Anthropology* 1, no. 3 (2013).

migrants."[8] Another manifestation of such politics of time can be found in "timing," the moment in which certain policies are installed. As Brux, Hilden, and Middelthon argue, the timing of the construction of fences after the "refugee crisis" in 2015 can be understood as a clear example of a temporal element in the "spectacle of enforcement of the border," to use an expression of Nicholas de Genova.[9]

One other important means for the temporal control over the entry and presence of people on a certain territory is the categorization of different types of migrants. For all of these categories, different sets of rules and regulations apply, and time plays a pivotal role in this form of governance. Hannah Arendt and Michel Foucault have argued that modern forms of power and politics should be conceived as control by means of the administration, categorization, and calculation of human life. In his lectures at the Collège de France, Foucault famously dubs this form of governmental power "governmentalité," a new form of power that aims to manage the life of a population. Whereas traditional forms of power controlled its subjects by means of the threat of death, or the direct control over the physical body, the modern subject is controlled by taking charge of the life of the population. This entails the control and study of processes, which occur over a period of time, and not so much the mere control of individual bodies.[10]

In migration law, such temporal control by categorization is rather apparent.[11] Residence rights and entitlements are not equally distributed among everyone present on a certain territory. As Linda Bosniak has argued, one of the main forms of immigration control takes place on the territory, and to a lesser extent at the territorial borders. This immigration control takes the form of differentiation between different legal statuses.

> The operation of a state's immigration admissions and citizenship allocation system produces an array of statuses among members of the society's population, so that at any given time, some people are citizens and some are Aliens, and among Aliens, there are various status locations assigned by the state. The result is that different people in the society enjoy different sets of right and recognition by virtue of their legal status and assignment.[12]

In this chapter, I demonstrate that this legal differentiation often makes use of time. I focus on two pivotal conceptions of time in this book, clock time and human time, and investigate how they are used in law to gain control over the processes of migrants living on a territory.

The Success of Clock Time

We live in what Robert Hassan has called "clock time modernity," in which life is ruled by an unambiguous and dominating conception of clock time, which is the time of money,

[8] Tazzioli, "The Temporal Borders of Asylum: Temporality of Control in the EU Border Regime," p. 17.

[9] Brux, Hilden, and Middelthon, "Klokka Tikker, Tiden Gar."

[10] K. Braun, "Biopolitics and Temporality in Arendt and Foucault," *Time and Society* 16, no. 1 (2007), p. 11. See also, Reneman and Stronks, "What Are They Waiting For?"

[11] This phenomenon of the "temporal border" is part of the what Ayelet Shachar has dubbed the phenomenon of the "the shifting border," see Shachar, *The Shifting Border*, and also Tazzioli, "The Temporal Borders of Asylum." It will be further discussed in the Conclusion of this book.

[12] L. Bosniak, "Being Here: Ethical Territoriality and the Rights of Immigrants," *Theoretical Inquiries in Law* 8, no. 2 (2007), p. 390.

industry, and technology. Hassan argues in his book *Empires of Speed* that the clock has created its own temporal reality since the Industrial Revolution.

> What does the clock do? Through its mathematical gearing system, its design-function is to "measure" time in society. However like trying to measure the waves on the seas, or clouds in the skies, or memories in the consciousness, and to attempt to measure these as regular and rhythmic sequences, it measures what cannot be measured in such a way. It slices the diverse timescapes of cultures, of societies and of the natural environment into uniform, precise and predictable bits that we can supposedly count and measure and value like pennies in a coin cylinder.[13]

Disguising itself as the measurement of time, the clock transforms what it supposedly measures. As such, the clock functions as a powerful tool to regulate and coordinate actions of individuals and groups in society.

Clock time is therefore perfectly apt for usage in law. It is uniform, precise, and has a predictable character that allows clock time to be used as a quantifiable good in regulations. If one thinks for example about the difficulties we would encounter if a criterion like "maturity" was used as prerequisite for people to be able to vote in elections, one would immediately grasp the advantage of a straightforward age criterion. Everyone has an age, or at least can be assigned one, so an age criterion allows for a simple application in law. Clock time allows for quantification so that it can be applied universally as common currency, as Elizabeth Cohen explains in her book *The Political Value of Time*.[14] Such quantification provides a clarity and logic to processes that are intangible, or at least very difficult to grasp. Take a term for naturalization, almost every law on naturalization will use a time criterion, often five years of residence, as a prerequisite for becoming a national. Such a criterion might refer to becoming "rooted" as a migrant, or the social integration or assimilation in the host society. One of the advantages of a time criterion for naturalization is that it refers to such processes without pinning down the exact relationship. Since everyone seems to accept that rootedness and integration have something to do with lapse of time, the abstraction from the individual processes in general time criteria works very well in law and politics. The processes might be intangible but they happen in time and the reference to lapse of time makes it more tangible. Moreover, it is precisely this abstraction from individual life stories that provides time with its objective and impartial character. As Hassan points out, the clock measures what cannot be measured in such a way; it transforms the variable into the invariable. And it is precisely this characteristic that provides the clock the force of organizational logic. Every individual life might be unique, just as every life on a certain territory might develop at a different pace or in specific directions, but all of these different lives surely share the fact that they happen in time and that they can be translated into hours and days of clock time.

[13] Hassan, *Empires of Speed*, p. 51.

[14] Cohen argues that there are five attributes of time that make it an ideal means for valuation and transaction over rights in liberal democratic states.

> These are: (1) ideas about time are embedded in contingent social circumstances and histories that are of particular relevance to the formation of national communities; (2) time can be scientifically measured and quantified ; (3) time's quantification lends it an air of scientific objectivity and impartiality; (4) the connection of time's supposed impartiality with the appearance of fair, or even egalitarian political rules; (5) time is able to be both embedded and appear objective, while most other means of valuation are either on or the other. (p. 104)

Furthermore, this quantification of time by means of the clock not only allows for simple application of the general rule to an individual case, it also permits commensuration by means of calculation. Calculation on the basis of time in legal criteria is the ultimate example of how a legal decision about the life of a human being can be detached from the singularities of that particular life, while still referring to it. It puts varied and undetermined processes into common, comparable criteria, which allow for political calculation to obtain different policy aims.

The Dutch policy for the withdrawal of residence status for public order offenses might serve as an illustration for the advantages of calculations on the basis of time. Breach of public order is a generally accepted ground for the withdrawal of residence status.[15] A residence status is in this sense always conditional: if the migrant commits a (severe) crime, the status can be revoked. In addition to the conditionality, however, another principle is at work in whether a residence status can be revoked. Generally, it is the case that the longer the migrant resides on a territory, the more difficult it is to withdraw a residence status. One could say that the conditionality of the migrant's residence status diminishes over time. When precisely a breach of public order is severe enough to withdraw residence status, however, is a difficult question that leads to a complex balancing of the different interests at hand. The best illustration for the complexity of such a balancing exercise can be found in the case-law of the European Court of Human Rights (ECtHR) on Article 8 ECHR (European Convention on Human Rights) in judgments concerning the withdrawal of residence status for breach of public order.[16]

This Dutch policy is a good example of such a calculation because it has replaced this multifaceted balancing exercise with a rather straightforward form of time calculation. The question whether a migrant can lose a residence permit because of a criminal offense depends in the Netherlands since 1990 on the application of the so-called sliding scale. This sliding scale is, in fact, a chart in which the relation between time and crime is objectified. The chart consists of two axes – the horizontal axis representing the quantity of time lawfully spent in the country, and the vertical axis reflecting the seriousness of the crime as expressed by the length of the unconditional part of the imposed sentence. If the unconditional part of the prison sentence falls within the criterion of the sliding scale, the residence permit of the migrant may be withdrawn or not renewed. So, for example, if a migrant is convicted of shoplifting, this would be enough to withdraw residence status after a residence of one year but not after a residence of fifteen years. The sliding scale therefore objectifies the legal judgment by means of time. This allows, in theory at least, for general, simple, and equal application of the norm to different cases.

The calculation with clock time serves yet another political and legal value; not only does it make an individual process tangible and generalized, it moreover makes policy and policy changes very visible. The history of the Dutch sliding scale may again serve as a good example of this.[17] The sliding scale was created in 1990 for two reasons. First, it was the result of an urge for legal certainty and legal equality. These principles were apparently not

[15] See, for example, ECHR November 2, 2001, *Boultif* v. *Switzerland*, 54273/00 or Article 12 Directive 2003/109.

[16] ECHR November 2, 2001, *Boultif* v. *Switzerland*, 54273/00; ECHR October 18, 2006, *Üner* v. *the Netherlands*, 46410/99; ECHR June 23, 2008, *Maslov* v. *Austria*, 1638/03.

[17] M. C. Stronks, "Een Bijna Ongebrijdelde Beteugeling van de Tijd: Een Analyse van Aanscherpingen van de Glijdende Schaal," *Nederlands Juristenblad*, no. 34 (2013).

well served with the open public order norm at that time in force and in particular with the highly case-based and individualistic application of that norm.[18] The sliding scale was meant to fill in the gaps. It was considered to be a simple norm with a general application, and was meant to cover every imaginable situation. Second, with the systematic approach of the sliding scale, the legal position of the migrant became much stronger. The applicable norms stipulated very clearly when migrants could lose their status. Consequently, if the said norm was not met, the residence permit would not be withdrawn. In addition, the norms of the sliding scale were, in general, much more generous for the migrant than in the situation before 1990.

Within the period 2001–12, however, the sliding scale was altered six times, with the most notable changes being the modifications of 2002, 2010, and 2012. It became much easier to withdraw a given residence permit when the migrant committed a criminal offense. Lighter trespassing of the criminal law was brought under the application of the sliding scale and a separate scale was introduced for recidivists. The extent of the change is best visible if the last step of the 1990s sliding scale is compared with that of the recidivist scale of 2012. In the 1990s, only drug trafficking with an imposed unconditional sentence of eight years or more (ninety-six months) constituted a possibility to withdraw the status after more than fifteen years of legal residence. In 2012, every imposed unconditional sentence of a little more than one year (fourteen months) was sufficient to take away legal status from recidivists who legally resided more than fifteen years in the Netherlands. Nonetheless, the most sweeping change in the policy was the removal of the twenty-year clause – the clause that made it impossible to withdraw status after residence of more than twenty years. As a result of this change, the conditionality of residence was no longer limited by an end term. Potentially, migrants could lose their residence status at any time, irrespective of how long they had already resided in the country.[19]

Certainly, this changed attitude toward criminality of migrants is part of a broader development in (European) migration law, and not typically Dutch.[20] However, another way to look at this history is to see that the time criteria of this policy instrument were discovered to be a rather easy way to change rules and regulations to adjust migration policy.[21] With a simple change of the terms of the sliding scale, a more restrictive policy was achieved. Just as migrants who breach public order are an easy target for a restrictive and firm migration policy is, clock time is a likely candidate for simple and visible changes of

[18] Interestingly enough, the case-law of the European Court of Human Rights on the withdrawal of residence status of long-term residing migrants is similarly accused of being arbitrary, see e.g., C. Steinorth, "Üner v the Netherlands : Expulsion of Long-Term Immigrants and the Right to Respect for Private and Family Life," *Human Rights Law Review* 8, no. 1 (2008); or see more mildly, Thym who writes "[t]he assessment of individual cases under the proportionality test was never supposed to resemble a mathematical formula," D. Thym, "Residence as de Facto Citizenship? Protection of Long-Term Residence under Article 8 ECHR," in *Human Rights and Immigration* (Oxford: Oxford University Press, 2014), pp. 126. In his dissenting opinion to the case of *Boughanemi* v. *France*, Judge Martens notoriously dubbed the case-law "a lottery" and a "source of embarrassment for the Court," see ECHR March 27, 1996, *Boughanemi* v *France*, 16/1995/522/608, dissenting opinion Judge Martens, par. 4.

[19] The Dutch Council of State has recently filed a request for a preliminary ruling with the CJEU inquiring whether the changed Dutch policy to allow for withdrawal of residence status after twenty years of residence of Turkish nationals would be at odds with the "standstill-clause" of Article 13 Decision 1/80 of the earlier mentioned Association Agreement, CJEU (pending), *E & C*, C-402/21.

[20] Cpr. Griffiths, "The Changing Politics of Time in the UK Immigration System," pp. 52–3.

[21] Stronks, "Een Bijna Ongebrijdelde Beteugeling van de Tijd."

policies toward such an aim. One does not have to be an expert in migration law to understand that if residence status can still be withdrawn after ten years based on a single conviction of shop lifting, this is more restrictive than reducing the period to the first five years of residence. If you compare such time criteria with a material assessment of the relevant interests at stake, the advantages of time criteria come clearly to the fore.

My favorite example of the success of clock time in migration law, however, stems from the EU Long-Term Residence Directive.[22] It is in this example that all of the virtues of legal time become apparent. In fact, it serves as an example of the use of clock time, while it can also function as bridge to the next discussion on the role of human time. Migrants who lawfully reside in one of the Member States of the EU for a period of five continuous years can apply for Long-Term Resident Status. Such a status is stronger, for there are fewer possibilities to withdraw the said permit. Migrants who reside on the territory for temporary purposes are excluded from the application of the Directive.

The CJEU has explained in the case of *Mangat Singh* why such residence falls outside the scope of the Long-Term Resident Directive. Whilst the residence of temporary migrants is lawful and of a possibly continuous nature,

> [the temporary residence] does not prima facie reflect any intention on the part of such nationals to settle on a long-term basis in the territory of the Member States. Thus, Article 3(2)(e) of Directive 2003/109 excludes from the scope of that directive, residence "on temporary grounds." Such grounds imply residence by a third-country national in the Member State concerned which is not long term.[23]

Nevertheless, the Court hastens to add, this does not preclude a continuous residence. After all, intentions might change, someone who intends to stay temporarily today, might wish to reside permanently tomorrow, and vice versa.

The Long-Term Residence Directive facilitates this change and does so by means of a fine example of time calculation. Students fall outside the scope of the Directive since their residence is deemed to be temporary. However, it is perfectly conceivable that they acquire another residence status after graduation because they start working or are granted a status on the basis of family reunification. In such a scenario, their temporary status after lapse of time could turn out to be more permanent than initially intended. Based on the general rule, their residence during study would not count for the five-year period of the Directive since such temporary residence does not count. If this temporary residence turns out to be nontemporary after all due to acquiring a nontemporary residence title, this retrospectively influences the previous period of presumed temporary residence. Article 4, paragraph 2, second subparagraph, stipulates that in such cases, the earlier period of residence for study purposes does count, although only half of the periods can be taken into account.

Clock time has many virtues, so much has become clear: it is seemingly objective; it is general while it refers to individual lives; it allows for quantification and calculation; and it has a certain clarity and visibility that are appealing for transparent and understandable policy making. Yet, next to clock time, another form of time is at work in law. The example of the temporary student changing his mind about his future can again help to pinpoint this form of time; this reference to human time.

[22] Directive 2003/109. [23] CJEU October 18, 2012, *Mangat Singh*, C-502/10, paragraphs 47–8.

The Function of Human Time in Law

The student who finds a job after graduation and changes his mind about the future (or always intended to aim for prolonged stay) serves as a nice example of time calculation in the Long-Term Residence Directive. Nonetheless, his case can just as well function as an illustration of the meaning of the adjective "temporary" in law. What does it mean when a residence is deemed to be temporary? Trying to answer that question is a good way to illustrate the use of human time in law.

It is important to observe from the outset that the adjective "temporary" does not relate well to clock time. As mentioned in the Introduction, clock time is standardized, which has the advantage that it serves as an objective standard. It can be applied to a migrant in order to establish at which moment in clock time they arrived and how long the residence subsequently took. However, purely on the basis of clock time, one cannot establish whether a certain residence is temporary. Certainly, the residence of the migrant can be established as temporary when the migrant leaves the territory without intention to return and thereby proves the residence was retrospectively temporary. The point is, however, that even such a perspective of temporary residence presumes human time because it presumes that their presence in the territory has become a definite part of their past, since they no longer reside and will not reside there in the future. Temporariness is therefore primarily a question of the temporality of human time, the time of someone with its past, present, and future as perceived at a certain moment in time.

The strain between temporariness and clock time becomes even more apparent if one thinks about the meaning of temporariness when the migrant has *not* left the territory. It is clear from the aforementioned example that residence can be retrospectively deemed as temporary, but can temporariness also be prospective and relate to the future? This is an urgent question, since the law uses temporary as a distinguishing category for migrants present within territory. Categories such as temporary, permanent, or long-term would be inoperable if one would have to wait until the actual migration of the migrant to another country. Migration law therefore uses a prospective conception of temporary. Such a prospective understanding cannot be objectified in a similar vein to the retrospective conception of temporariness. So, what determines when some residence is deemed to be temporary and other residence is deemed nontemporary in the future? Rainer Bauböck has argued that, indeed, different meanings of temporary should be discerned. He discusses several prospective understandings of temporary; the most important being for this discussion: subjectively intended; collectively expected; and legally prescribed.[24] It becomes apparent that there is a complex interplay at stake between these three perceptions in the meaning of temporary residence.

The temporary character of time in the territory relates in the first place to the supposed intention of the migrant that is attributed to their residence permit. This intention does not exclusively refer to the intention of the migrant. Obviously, the intention of the migrant plays a role, after all they choose to migrate to the country and to apply for a particular residence permit (work, asylum, family reunification, study, work as an *au pair*, etc.). Moreover, what will actually happen in the future very much depends on the intention of

[24] Bauböck also discerns "morally justified" and "demographically objective," the latter being the retrospective variant that I have just described. R. Bauböck, "Temporary Migrants, Partial Citizenship and Hypermigration," *Critical Review of International Social and Political Philosophy* 14, no. 5 (2011), p. 670.

the migrant, which may change. Whatever is intended at a particular moment can change in the future because the migrant may change initial plans. It is perfectly conceivable that a migrant, who has gained a strong residence permit, decides after a couple of years to migrate again and settle somewhere else; just as someone with a temporary permit (e.g. study) might decide to settle (find a job or fall in love) despite an initial plan to leave. Therefore, the subjective intention of the migrant is a rather unreliable proxy to predict the future. It is for this reason that migration law has a construction relating to the temporary character of the migrant's presence on the basis of a reasonable expectation of the future, instead of a purely subjective intention.

In fact, this is present in the previous argument of the CJEU in *Mangat Singh*: the residence of migrants who stay for temporary purposes does not reflect any prima facie intention on the part of these migrants to settle on a long-term basis. This does not imply an inquiry into the actual intention of these migrants, it is a constructed legal expectation. This reasonable expectation comes close to Bauböck's "collectively expected." It is the legal attempt to construct a reasonable expectation based on the objective of the visit. If such a goal is temporary, if the end of the stay is implied in the goal, then the time of residence is expected to be temporary as well. If a migrant comes to work as a seasonal worker, for a particular study, or for temporary protection, these forms of residence have a (more or less) clear end point. Therefore, these forms of temporary residence are exempted from the Long-Term Residence Directive.

Consequently, what can "temporary residence" mean? It implies a prospective qualification of the time a migrant wants to spend on the territory. Such an expectation is necessary since it is not just clock time in the territory, it is the time *someone* will spend in the territory. Mere clock time will not suffice as qualification of their presence as (non) temporary, for it implies a temporal understanding of the time of the migrant. The qualification refers to the future of the migrant and this reflects a complicated interplay between objectively expected, subjectively intended, and legally prescribed.

This example serves not only to show how human time is at work in migration law, it also demonstrates how human time is used to make categorizations between different migrants. It would, in other words, be too simple a conclusion to say that the success of time in migration law is purely based on its use of clock time. Although the virtues of clock time for application in law are apparent, in the end, it is the human time of the migrant that is the object of governance. It is, in fact, in the interplay between clock time and human time that we can identify different forms of temporal differentiations: legal distinctions to govern the presence of migrants on the territory based on their human time.

Techniques of Temporal Differentiation

As discussed in the introduction of this chapter, the governance of migrants present within a given territory makes use of intricate forms of differentiations – differentiations that are often based on time. Since the presence of people on a territory is not static but a process that develops over time, I argue here that these processes lend themselves for differentiation. I discern four differentiations that make use of time: differentiation based on temporality; differentiation based on deadlines; differentiation by qualification of time; and procedural differentiation. All four sorts will be discussed and it will become apparent that in many of the examples, multiple forms of temporal differentiation are at work.

Clearly, there is overlap between them, differentiation on the basis of temporality is for example an obvious form of qualification, whilst procedural sorts of differentiation often make use of deadlines. The point is however to show that their functioning makes a different usage of time, and the interplay between clock and human time.

Temporality

Bridget Anderson has observed that the United Nations' (UN's) definition of who constitutes a migrant is one of time. The UN data on global migration define a migrant as "a person who moves to a country other than that of his or her usual residence for a period of twelve months or more so that the country of destination effectively becomes his or her new country of usual residence." What matters is time away from the usual residence and the length of time planned to stay.[25] Temporality – the distinction between past, present, and future – is pivotal in such a definition; not only does it rely on an estimation of the length of the visit, the qualification of "usual residence" is based on an estimation of past, present, and future. Temporality is not just used for the definition of who constitutes a migrant, in migration law it is used to further categorize migrants and to differentiate between their entitlements, or to use Elizabeth Cohen's words, to "discriminate" by means of "temporal boundaries."[26]

Just as differentiations can be made focussing on clock time (e.g. five years of residence before long-term residence status), it is possible to categorize based on temporality.[27] As already seen in the previous paragraph, based on the distinction between temporary, nontemporary, and permanent residence, differentiations can be made between different forms of migration and different entitlements can be attached to the respective categories. Seasonal workers, *au pairs*, and students are deemed to reside temporarily on the territory and are therefore excluded from the stronger residence status of the Long-Term Residence Directive; just as refugees receive temporary protection until the situation in their country of origin has become safe enough to return.[28] The crux in this form of differentiation is that distinctions are based on the past or the future of the migrant, at a certain moment in time.

[25] Anderson, "And About Time Too . . . Migration Documentation, and Temporalities."

[26] Cohen, *The Political Value of Time*, p. 60.

[27] This aspect of temporality – the relationship between past, present, and future – is one of the central questions of the phenomenology of time in the work of, for example, Edmund Husserl, Martin Heidegger, and Merleau-Ponty, see for a helpful introduction to this question, Hoy, *The Time of Our Lives*, pp. 41–95. In the next chapter, this question will be further discussed as the problem of extension in the work of Bergson and Heidegger.

[28] The most obvious example of this latter category of temporariness is the Temporary Protection Directive, Directive 2001/55, a directive that has never been implemented, see Ineli-Ciger, *Temporary Protection in Law and Practice*, pp. 149–93. Interestingly enough, the new proposal for a regulation addressing situations of crisis and force majeure in the field of migration and asylum presented by the European Commission proposes to repeal the Temporary Protection Directive and introduce "immediate protection," see for a first discussion of the differences, M. Ineli-Ciger, "What a Difference Two Decades Make? The Shift from Temporary to Immediate Protection in the New European Pact on Asylum and Migration," *EU Migration Blog* (2020), https://eumigrationlawblog.eu/what-a-difference-two-decades-make-the-shift-from-temporary-to-immediate-protection-in-the-new-european-pact-on-asylum-and-migration/. For a concise discussion of temporary protection in the USA, see N. Lori, "Migration, Time and the Shift to Autocracy," in *The Shifting Border*, eds. A. Shachar and P. Niesen, pp. 118–38 (Manchester: Manchester University Press, 2020).

Seasonal workers receive a temporary residence status because the aim and prospect of this form of residence is that it will stop when the season has come to an end. This form of temporal differentiation therefore always presupposes a moment in time when a prediction of the future (or the assessment of the past) is made. At this moment, the future is fixated by means of legal categorization, which is linked to certain residence entitlements.

While such temporal differentiation is based on the qualification of the future, it can endure long-term, as can be exemplified by the case of the Ghanaian woman with which this book commenced but also with the earlier mentioned case of *Mangat Singh* before the CJEU. Mr. Singh, an Indian national, was granted an "ordinary fixed-period residence permit" in the Netherlands, the validity of which was limited to the exercise of an activity as a spiritual leader or religious teacher for a fixed period of time. The permit was first granted for one year and subsequently multiple times extended for a fixed period of an extra three years. After Mr. Singh had resided for five years, he requested Long-Term Resident status, under the Long-Term Residence Directive. This was, however, rejected; the Dutch government qualified the residence as temporary because its duration was "formally limited" in the sense of Article 3(2)(e) of the Long-Term Residence Directive. In the meantime, the government kept prolonging the said residence permit, therewith precluding that Mr. Singh would gain a stronger residence status while remaining lawfully within the territory. In other words, Mr. Singh was kept in long-term temporariness, and as political philosopher Michael Walzer puts it in *Spheres of Justice*: "the purpose of their status is to prevent them from improving their condition."[29]

Even though the CJEU ruled in this case that this form of long-term temporariness is not allowed under EU law, the case of Mr. Singh still serves as an excellent example of the differentiating effect of temporal governance by means of temporality. It is clear from this example that the relevant moment in time is the moment that the residence status is being granted, the expectation at that moment determines whether the residence is qualified as temporary or nontemporary. It is this expectation of the future of the migrant that is the locus of temporal differentiation. And in an ultimate form, it implies that the qualification as temporary can be renewed time and again, keeping the de facto long-term residence temporary.

A related but slightly different example of the central role of temporariness in the qualification of presence within a territory is the case-law relating to the so-called Europe-route. The example of Mr. Singh explicates how the assessment of the future of the migrant is linked to a certain moment in time, after which the future remains unaltered. The example of the Europe-route shows how temporality is used to qualify presence within a given territory. One of the fundamental rights of EU citizens is their right to move and reside freely within the territory of one of the Member States of the EU. This right can be found in Article 21 TFEU (Treaty for the Functioning of the European Union), and the Citizenship Directive (Directive 2004/38) aims to facilitate and strengthen the exercise of this right. One of the important rights that follows from this Directive is the right to family reunification with a third-country national family member. This right is a derived right, which means that it follows from the exercise of freedom of movement by an EU citizen.[30] Even though it is not an autonomous right for the third-country national, it clearly is a

[29] M. Walzer, *Spheres of Justice* (New York: Basic Books, 1983), p. 58.
[30] CJEU November 8, 2012, *Iida*, C-40/11, paragraphs 66–7.

strong entitlement, often more lenient than national rules for family reunification. Importantly, the right to reunite with a family member does not apply when the EU citizen remains in the country of their nationality. After all, the right is attached to the freedom of movement of the citizen. Yet, the CJEU argued that if the EU citizen was not able to bring their family member to the other Member State *and* back to the Member State of their nationality, this could be an obstacle to the EU citizen exercising their freedom of movement in the first place. For this reason, the CJEU has ruled that when an EU citizen has resided in a Member State other than the one where they are a national, the family member also has a derived right to reside in the Member State of the EU citizen's nationality after they return from their residence abroad.[31]

It was feared by some Member States that this could be a way to circumvent more restrictive rules for family reunification.[32] Such construction is called the Europe-route and it implies that residence in another Member State would be enough to exempt the family from national rules for family reunification. The decisive question to apply the lenient European rules in such cases is: *When* is residence of an EU citizen in another Member State of the EU long enough to qualify for this derived right of EU law? In other words, the question of temporariness of residence has become nothing less than the boundary between national and European law.

This question could have been answered merely by reference to a clock time criterion: after a certain period of time, residence would be long enough to activate the derived residence rights for family members. Yet, the Court has clarified in the case of O and B that the relevant criterion is that "only where the residence of the Union citizen in the host Member State has been sufficiently genuine so as to enable that citizen to create or strengthen family life in that Member State."[33] Residence on the basis of Article 6 of the Citizenship Directive, which is restricted to a period of three months, does not reflect an intention of the EU citizen to settle in the host Member State. Residence on the basis of Article 7, however, is in principle evidence of settling and therefore of the aforementioned genuine residence. Yet, it is for the national government to determine whether the EU citizen has settled, therewith proving that the said residence is sufficiently genuine to create or strengthen family life in the host state. Such an assessment of whether residence is sufficiently genuine is reminiscent of the earlier mentioned UN definition of "usual residence," or a notion like "habitual residence" that can be found back in tax law, social security law, and international private law. This criterion therewith implies an assessment of the future of the migrant, or upon return of an assessment of whether the previous residence was sufficiently genuine in order to take the family member back to the home country of the EU citizen.

These examples show that temporality – the past, present, and future – of the migrant are used to differentiate the presence of migrants within a certain territory. It requires time and again an assessment of the future and/or the past of the individual at a particular moment.

31 CJEU July 7, 1992, *Surinder Singh*, C-370/90; CJEU December 11, 2007, *Eind*, C-291/05.

32 H. Kroeze, "Distinguishing between Use and Abuse of EU Free Movement Law: Evaluating Use of the 'Europe-Route' for Family Reunification to Overcome Reverse Discrimination," in *European Citizenship under Stress*, eds. N. Cambien, D. Kochenov, and E. Muir (Leiden: Martinus Nijhoff, 2020), p. 227; E. Spaventa, "Family Rights for Circular Migrants and Frontier Workers: O and B, and S and G," *Common Market Law Review* 52, no. 3 (2015).

33 CJEU March 12, 2014, *O & B*, C-456-12, paragraph 51.

Moreover, it has become clear that this temporal differentiation aims at the process of the migrant's presence within a given territory. Distinctions are made based on the past and future of the migrant within a certain territory to differentiate legal entitlements.

There is, however, another sort of application of temporality that deserves to be discussed; notably, the usage of the "present or actual danger" criterion within the case-law of the CJEU in public order cases.[34] In this line of case-law, temporality is used not so much to differentiate the presence within a territory such as in the cases of *Mangat Singh* and the Europe-route, but instead the *behavior* of the migrant is the locus of differentiation.

Article 28 of the Citizenship Directive stipulates that Member States may restrict the freedom of movement of EU citizens on grounds of public policy and public security. In cases in which an EU citizen has been convicted of criminal offenses, they might be expelled to their country of origin. Such a decision should be proportionate and based exclusively on the conduct of the individual concerned. Moreover, and importantly, mere previous convictions do not constitute grounds for taking such measures; "the personal conduct of the individual concerned must represent a genuine, present and sufficiently serious threat affecting one of the fundamental interests of society." This criterion has come to be known as the "present or actual danger criterion"; the relevant assessment is not whether there was in the past a sufficiently serious and genuine threat, there should still be a danger that still exists in the present of the legal decision. *When* is such a danger still present?

The CJEU has held in the case of Orfanopoulos and Oliveri that the time that elapsed between the decision to expel the person concerned and that of the review of the competent courts should be taken into account when considering whether the danger is still present.[35] What happens in that period of time is therewith determinative for the question of whether there still exists an actual danger. If the person reoffends, this is obviously indicative that there still exists a danger, especially if the time that lapsed since the last crime is relatively short. Yet, the seriousness of the offense is also an important criterion to take into account. As we will see in Chapter 2, some offenses can be so disturbing for society – such as war crimes or crimes against humanity – that the danger will not easily diminish over a (long) period of time. Yet, the Court held already in its judgment in Bouchereau in 1977 that a previous criminal conviction cannot in itself justify an expulsion measure, the relevant question is whether there exists in the individual concerned "a propensity to act in the same way in the future."[36] Are there any positive signs of reintegration, reports from psychiatrists, or indications of structurally changed behavior such as the end of a drug addiction? Such elements can be used as substantiation of the absence of a propensity to reoffend. This implies that the assessment constitutes an estimation of the future – of the risk the person constitutes for society. Temporality is used to pinpoint the present moment, in which a qualification of the future risk is being made, this qualified future serves to differentiate between those whose residence status can be withdrawn or not. Whereas in the previous

[34] Also, the European Court of Human Rights has held in certain public order cases under Article 8 ECHR that the proportionality assessment was "ultimately designed to help evaluate the extent to which the applicant can be expected to cause disorder or to engage in criminal activities," ECHR June 23, 2008, *Maslov* v. *Austria*, 1638/03, paragraph 70. The case-law is, however, not consistent on this point, only in eleven of fifty-eight cases does it explicitly refer to this danger assessment, see H. van Oort, "De Strafrechtelijk Veroordeelde Vreemdeling en Artikel 8 EVRM," *Asiel&Migrantenrecht*, no. 5 (2020).

[35] CJEU April 29, 2004, *Orfanopoulos and Oliveri*, C-482/01 and C-493/01, paragraphs 78–81.

[36] CJEU October 27, 1977, *Bouchereau*, C-30-77, paragraph 29.

examples, presence within the territory was the locus for differentiation by means of temporality, the case-law on the "present danger" criterion shows that temporality can also be used to differentiate between acceptable and unacceptable behavior.

Deadlines

Probably the most frequently used form of temporal differentiation is the one based on deadlines. For example, the residence status of family members often remains dependent on that of the sponsor for a period of five years (e.g. Article 15 of the Family Reunification Directive). Similarly, it is possible to allow family reunification only after the sponsor has first lawfully resided a fixed period of time on the territory (e.g. two years in the Family Reunification Directive). These are examples of what Elizabeth Cohen calls "countdown deadlines," a type of temporal boundary in which limitations are linked to two dates by a precise quantity of time.[37] In the example of the dependent status of the family member, the former date would be the acquisition of the dependent residence status as family member, the latter would be the fixed amount of lapsed years before the family member may apply for an autonomous status.

Countdown deadlines can be used to regulate certain entitlements, such as the earlier mentioned autonomous status, a long-term resident status, or naturalization, or for procedural differentiations (see further "Procedures"). Just as they can be linked to the grant of a (stronger) residence status or other entitlement, they can be used to end certain entitlements. Residence permits are always first granted for a certain period of time, after which, the entitlement if not renewed or changed, ceases to exist. Another example of a countdown deadline is the "period of voluntary departure" that can be granted to a migrant who no longer has authorization to stay within the territory. Article 7 of the Returns Directive stipulates that as a general rule, return decisions shall provide for an "appropriate period" for voluntary departure of between seven and thirty days. Another example of a fixed time limit by means of a countdown deadline is the maximum period of immigration detention, which is set at eighteen months (Article 15 (6)) in the Returns Directive. It is interesting to contrast this with the conclusion of the ECtHR in the case of *J. N. v. the United Kingdom* that Article 5 (1) of the ECHR does not require states to be contracted to establish a maximum period of immigration detention.[38] In other words, the justified duration of detention can be based on a countdown deadline just as well as on a review of all of the particularities of the individual case. I will return to this distinction in the next chapter when discussing the formal/material problem in referring to processes.

[37] Cohen, *The Political Value of Time*, p. 56.

[38] ECHR May 19, 2016, *J. N. v. the United Kingdom*, 37289/12, paragraphs 90–3; the Court concludes

> It is clear that the existence or absence of time-limits is one of a number of factors which the Court might take into consideration in its overall assessment of whether domestic law was "sufficiently accessible, precise and foreseeable" (in other words, whether there existed "sufficient procedural safeguards against arbitrariness"). However, in and of themselves they are neither necessary nor sufficient to ensure compliance with the requirements of Article 5 § 1(f) (see, for example, Gallardo Sanchez, cited above, § 39, and Auad, cited above, § 131, in which the Court made it clear that even if fixed time-limits were complied with, it would still find an applicant's detention to be in breach of Article 5 § 1(f) if deportation was not pursued with due diligence). (paragraph 90)

In their functioning countdown deadlines make use of both clock and human time, albeit, that the former is most prominent. They stipulate that after a certain amount of clock time, a legal effect occurs, whilst this obviously implies the lapse of human time, such deadlines are generally not linked to specific periods of human time (e.g. first five years of the migrants life, or the time after the age of retirement). Because such countdown deadlines are expressed in terms of clock time, they can be repeated. The time for naturalization, for example, can start anew, in case someone has left the territory or when there is a period of unlawful residence.

Alongside "countdown deadlines" Cohen distinguishes yet another variant of deadlines: the "single moment deadlines" – deadlines based on a fixed, single moment in time. The most obvious example of such a temporal boundary is the acquisition of nationality at birth based on either ius soli or ius sanguinis principles. In the former, the child receives the nationality of the place of birth, in the latter, it receives nationality from the parents. Such a deadline is the basis for what Ayelet Shachar has criticized as the "birthright lottery", in which birthright determines the future of a child from the single moment of birth.[39] With such single-moment deadlines, the moment in time is merely expressed in terms of human time, which implies that it is not only an individual deadline but moreover unrepeatable. Also, the distinction between minor/adult can be seen as a single-moment boundary.[40] Single-moment deadlines can, however, also be expressed in terms of clock time (or to be precise, calendar time). An illustration of such a single moment deadline is the temporal clause in the Refugee Definition, which initially determined that refugee protection was restricted to events occurring before January 1, 1951 (this deadline was dropped after the Protocol of 1967). Equally, the date in which new laws and regulations come into force is an example of a single-moment deadline, after this particular moment, entitlements and procedures will be changed and have different legal effect. Just as rules regulating the acquisition of citizenship after the establishment of new sovereign borders make use of single-moment deadlines, such as in the case of the breakup of the Soviet Union into new states.[41] Another typical example of this form of deadline is "standstill agreements" in the Association Agreement that provide Turkish nationals residence rights. These standstill clauses provide that the EU Member States may not introduce new restrictions on the conditions to the right of establishment and the freedom to provide services and movement for workers after the date of entry into force of the legal measures. This implies that, for example, an application for a residence permit for a Turkish national starting a business should be dealt with according to the national immigration legislation of a Member State *as if it was still 1973.*[42]

A characteristic for single-moment deadlines that are expressed in terms of clock time is that they have a general application: the moment in time is fixed on a moment on the calendar. Single-moment deadlines are – both in human and clock time – to be

[39] A. Shachar, *The Birthright Lottery* (Cambridge, MA: Harvard University Press, 2009).

[40] See for a discussion of age assessment in European asylum law, E. Brouwer and R. Lanneau, "Age Assessment and the Protection of Minor Asylum Seekers: Time for a Harmonised Approach in the EU," *Refugee Law Initiative* (2020), https://rli.blogs.sas.ac.uk/2020/08/10/age-assessment-and-the-protection-of-minor-asylum-seekers-time-for-a-harmonised-approach-in-the-eu/.

[41] E. F. Cohen, "Citizenship and the Law of Time in the United States," *Duke Journal of Constitution Law & Public Policy* 53, no. 8 (2013).

[42] See further, P. Boeles et al., *European Migration Law* (Cambridge: Intersentia, 2014), pp. 118–26.

distinguished from countdown deadlines because they cannot be repeated. They make use of the arrow of time in both clock and human time to differentiate between a "before" and "after." Single-moment deadlines, Cohen argues, have limited normative potential because they cannot accommodate change, "they make no allowances for the fact that time, unlike land, is not static."[43] Countdown deadlines, on the contrary, leave room for more normative complexity, for they allow decisions to be made over a longer period of time. Such time is thought to have meaning, and the period of time allows the process of judgment and claim making to over many more points in time than the judgment affixed to one moment in time.[44]

In addition, the third form of deadline that Cohen describes are recurrent deadlines. Whilst countdown deadlines can be repeated, recurrent boundaries repeat themselves, "they create a schedule for the periodic re-evaluation and alteration of the boundary they demarcate."[45] Election cycles are based on such recurrent deadlines and are clearly linked to fixed periods of clock time. Recurrent deadlines can, however, also be linked to less specific periods of time. The Returns Directive requires, for example, that detention for the purpose of the removal of the unlawfully residing migrants "shall be reviewed at reasonable intervals of time" (Article 15 (3)).

The most interesting example of a recurrent deadline in the field of migration law is the amnesty or regularization for unlawfully residing migrants, which I will elaborately discuss in Chapter 3.

Qualification

Another form of temporal governance by means of differentiation is the qualification of time. We have already seen this at work in the discussion of temporality as a form of differentiation, after all, temporary residence is a form of qualification of residence. In temporal differentiation on the basis of temporality, however, the emphasis is on the usage of the past, present, and future of the migrant to differentiate. Yet, there is more to say about the usage of qualification, this is often used to qualify the presence of the migrant within a territory in other ways. One of the advantages of the use of time in law is that everyone has time. Humans are temporal beings, they live in time, and it is their individual time that is the focus of legal control. This does not serve to say, however, that legal time equates the simple lapse of individual human time. The deadlines that are often used in law almost never take time as unqualified, individual human time. Some form of qualification of time is always used to differentiate between different categories. The residence status of the family member, for example, remains dependent on that of their sponsor for a period of five years. Yet, this does not mean that mere lapse of time will make the status autonomous. As a rule, the relationship should not have been broken as a result of divorce or separation. One could say that it is not just time that should have lapsed, but marital or relational time.

A more informative example, however, of the seemingly endless possibilities of the qualification of time is the use of time in the Long-Term Residence Directive. Only time that is continuous qualifies for the Long-Term Resident Status. The period of five years may not be interrupted, stipulates Article 4, paragraph 1, as a general rule. This is a clear

[43] Cohen, *The Political Value of Time*, p. 55. [44] Ibid., p. 56. [45] Ibid., p. 58.

qualification of time, it is not merely the sum of years spent in the territory that counts for the Long-Term Residence Directive, they must have been consecutive years.

Recall Bridget Anderson's observation that what matters is time away from "usual residence." We already witnessed this differentiation of presence in discussing the genuine residence criterion in cases of the Europe-route, yet upon close scrutiny it turns outs that the continuity of residence can also be further qualified. On the basis of the wording of Article 4 one would think that continuous residence in the territory does not leave room for interruption by way of presence outside the territory. If the criterion of continuity would merely refer to clock time, it would be straightforward. The legal meaning of continuity appears, however, to be more complicated. Article 4, paragraph 3, stipulates that periods outside the territory shorter than six consecutive months, not exceeding in total ten months, do not interrupt the period of five years within the meaning of Article 4, paragraph 1. A migrant can therefore reside outside the territory (for holidays, visits, work, etc.) without this implying that the clock starts to tick all over again regarding their application for a long-term resident permit. Continuous time in the territory is accordingly defined as "uninterrupted not" or "not interrupted for too long."

Nonetheless, if a migrant is outside the territory, does that time compute for the countdown deadline of the long-term resident status? If a migrant leaves the territory for a four-week holiday, do these weeks count? Interestingly enough, the time of these non-intervals actually does count: they add to the period of five years, according to Article 4, paragraph 3. So, we have to discern the question of (non)interruption from the question of calculation. (Some) time on the outside does not interrupt time on the inside, and these noninterrupting intervals outside the territory even count as time on the inside. Longer time on the outside, however, does interrupt the continuous time on the inside and therefore makes the clock start ticking all over again.

It becomes, however, even more complicated. While the general rule of continuous time implies a form of "not often interrupted time," and these nonintervals count for the period of five years, there can be exceptions to this. In very exceptional circumstances of a temporary nature, Member States may agree that longer periods of absence of the territory will not interrupt the continuous time of five years (Article 4, paragraph 3, second subparagraph). In such cases, however, the relevant period of absence from the territory should not be taken into account in the calculation of the five-year period.

The possibilities for qualification of time are, in other words, endless. The example of the Long-Term Residence Directive shows that the detailed qualification of what constitutes as continuity can lead to complicated forms of time calculation. The quantifiable character of clock time lends itself for detailed regulations by means of qualification, which enables one to make very specific differentiations. Some time counts, while other time does not. However, the (dis)qualification of time does not have to be so meticulous, chunks of time can be entirely disqualified. If a migrant resides unlawfully on a territory, this time has not much legal value. Only after five years of lawful residence, for example, can a migrant apply for naturalization. I know of no country in the world that grants naturalization, no matter whether the time spent in the territory was lawful or unlawful.[46]

[46] Rubio-Marín has argued that a full version of the jus domicilii principle would entail the inclusion of migrants after a fixed period of time, no matter their legal status, see. R. Rubio-Marín, *Immigration as a Democratic Challenge: Citizenship and Inclusion in Germany and the United States* (Cambridge: Cambridge University Press, 2000).

A final example of qualification of time as unlawful stems from the case-law of the ECtHR. It is instructive because the ECtHR uses temporality to distinguish between precarious and unprecarous family life. In its case-law under Article 8, the Court has time and again held that Article 8 does not oblige states to respect an immigrant's choice of the country of their residence and to authorize family reunion in this territory. Nevertheless, there can be circumstances under which the family life should be protected in immigration cases, this will vary according to the particular circumstances of the case. One particularly important aspect is, however, "whether family life was created at a time when the persons involved were aware that the immigration status of one of them was such that the persistence of that family life within the host State would from the outset be precarious."[47] Where this is the case, the removal of the nonnational family member would be incompatible with Article 8 only in exceptional circumstances. Ever since the judgment of *Abdulaziz*, the Court has reiterated this formula as one of the important elements in the assessment whether family life is protected under the Convention. In this reasoning, the Court makes use of temporality, by using the moment that the family life started. When at that time the family members were aware that the persistence of the family life in the host country would be uncertain, this weighs heavily in the proportionality assessment. In other words, the court pinpoints a certain moment in the life of the migrant that is crucial for the evaluation of the weight of the subsequent family life. The awareness of the precarity of the immigration status at that time qualifies the family life as precarious, which implies that the removal of the family member would only be incompatible with Article 8 in exceptional circumstances.

Antedating

Antedating is a form of differentiation that could be defined as taking an earlier moment in time as the relevant legal moment. The most obvious example of this differentiation is the antedating of a residence permit. This implies that the starting moment of the permits antedates the moment of the legal decision to provide such a status, the best example of such is the antedating of the refugee permit to the moment of the application.

A second example of such differentiation relates to the relevant moment in time of the judicial decision. In continental traditions, such a distinction is, as mentioned when discussing the case of the Eritrean girl in the introduction of this chapter, often called the difference between ex nunc and ex tunc judgments. In an ex tunc judgment, the circumstances after the moment of the administrative decision cannot be taken into account in a subsequent judicial review, whilst in an ex nunc judgment, the relevant legal moment coincides with the moment of the judicial review. The case of the Eritrean girl serves as a good example. In the time taken for the procedure she had reached legal majority. The question of majority was of crucial importance for the case: as a child, she had the right to reunite with her parents, as an adult, such reunification would be difficult to achieve. The relevant moment in the procedure to establish the child's age was therefore pivotal. The CJEU held that only an ex tunc judgment would lead to a just

[47] ECHR June 28, 2011, *Nunez* v. *Norway*, 55597/09, paragraph 70, this criterion was to put to the fore for the first time in ECHR May 28, 1985, *Abdulaziz, Cabalis and Balkandali* v. *the United Kingdom*, 9214/80, 9473/81, and 9474/81, paragraph 68.

outcome, declaring that the girl was, legally speaking, seventeen years old (despite it being just before her twenty-second birthday).

Likewise, in the case-law of Article 8 ECHR, the question of the relevant moment plays an important role, especially regarding cases of expulsion of long-term residing migrants. Such cases often deal with migrants who have committed criminal offenses, after which the government withdrew their residence status. Immigration procedures, however, often encompass a long period of time, which implies that when the case reaches the (highest) court, a long time may have passed since the decision to withdraw the residence status. Since the moment of this decision, circumstances may have drastically changed. A migrant may have repeated their behavior or, on the contrary, have changed their life drastically for the better. Again, the relevant moment of the decision will be decisive for the outcome of such cases.[48]

This manipulation of the legally relevant moment is not only based on human time, it clearly refers to clock time as well. Actually, it is a revealing example of the intricate relationship between human time and clock time, as it implies a form of time traveling. As mentioned in the Introduction, it is possible to traverse a calendar in two directions because of its axial moment and the existence of a perceived human present. Because of this, it is possible to go "back" from the tangible present to the past and "forward" from the past to the present. This is what is at stake in the determination of the legally relevant moment with an ex nunc or ex tunc judgment. as a result of the calendar and the human "present" of the migrant, it is possible to go back to determine the relevant moment on the basis of an ex tunc assessment.

Procedures

The last sort of temporal differentiation that I would want to highlight is procedural differentiations. In the first place, there are several procedural deadlines, often countdown deadlines that stipulate when certain procedural steps should be taken – for example, procedures for filing an appeal or the limitations for submitting new evidence. Such procedural differentiations not only delimit the applicant, they can also circumscribe the power of the state. One can think of the maximum amount of time the government may take to come to a decision, or the maximum amount of time detention may take.

More complex, however, are differentiations based on acceleration and deceleration of procedure. Such differentiation is a clear example of temporal governance, as Marcelle Reneman and I have earlier contended elsewhere.[49] Governments frequently use the speed, and therewith the duration, of the procedure to distinguish between wanted and unwanted forms of mobility. The starkest example is the differentiation between mobility of EU citizens within the EU and the attempts of asylum seekers to reside in Europe.[50] The former can freely move and reside in Europe almost without any procedural temporalizations, the latter often has to wait years for a first decision on their asylum application. Waiting should, as Ruben Anderson argues, in such politics, not so much be perceived as a

[48] ECHR September 20, 2011, *A. A.* v. *the United Kingdom*, 8000/08, paragraph 67.

[49] Reneman and Stronks, "What Are They Waiting For?"

[50] Shachar, *The Shifting Border*; T. P. Spijkerboer, "The Global Mobility Infrastructure: Reconceptualising the Externalisation of Migration Control," *European Journal of Migration and Law* 20, no. 4 (2018).

by-product of state institutions and bureaucratic regulations but rather as a tactic, a management technique to control the inclusion and exclusion of migrants on a territory.[51] Or, as Pierre Bourdieu writes in his *Pascalian Meditations*, "[t]he all-powerful is he who does not wait but who makes others wait."[52] And indeed, the prerogative to let others wait seems an ultimate form of temporal governance; waiting implies a sort of submission, as Bourdieu claims. It can be argued that in European law, there is ample opportunity to prolong such waiting.[53]

Yet, to be accurate, one should add that the "all-powerful" is not just the one who makes others wait but the one who can determine the pace and therewith the duration of the procedures altogether. Making others wait might be an obvious example of temporal governance, yet suddenly accelerating procedures is clearly the other side of the same relationship between power and time. Such "frenzied time," as Melanie Griffiths calls it, is time that is experienced to accelerate quickly and rush out of control. Deportations and removals almost always entail such an accelerated sense of time,[54] as a consequence of which, effective legal remedies can become obsolete.

A good example of such frenzied time is the case of *De Souza Ribeiro* v. *France* before the ECtHR. Mr. De Souza Ribeiro was a man of Brazilian descent living with his family in French Guiana, a French overseas *département* in South America. He arrived in Guiana at the age of four in 1992, from 1996 to 2004 he attended primary and secondary school there, without having legal permission to reside in the territory. Whereas his family members lawfully resided in Guiana, he lacked a residence permit. In 2007, on February 25, to be precise, he was arrested at a road stop because he was unable to provide proof that his residence on French soil was legal. The same day, at 10 a.m., an administrative removal order and an administrative detention order were issued against him. On January 26, so the day after, at 3.11 p.m., De Souza Ribeiro sent two faxes to the Cayenne Administrative Court, one applying for judicial review of his removal in light of his personal and family life under Article 8 ECHR, the other an immediate suspension of the enforcement of the removal order. Only forty-nine minutes later, January 26, 2007 at 4 p.m., he was removed to Belim in Brazil. On the same day, the urgent application judge declared that the urgent application for suspension of the removal order to be devoid of purpose as De Souza Ribeiro had already been removed. This case shows how the sovereign's omnipotence not only becomes apparent in cases of waiting but just as well in cases of sudden acceleration.

Yet, this case can equally serve as an example of how acceleration can serve as a technique to regulate access to the law in the first place. It is precisely because of the sudden acceleration, the sudden enforcement of the law, that the migrant was withheld the

[51] Anderson, "Time and the Migrant Other."

[52] P. Bourdieu, *Pascalian Meditations*, trans. R. Nice (Stanford, CA: Stanford University Press, 2000), p. 228.

[53] Marcelle Reneman and I have argued that the Netherlands has used temporal governance to differentiate between asylum seekers with high chances of success and those with lower chances. The former have to wait a very long time, often longer than legally allowed, while the proceedings of the latter are prioritized and accelerated. We argue that law always leaves room for "temporal discretion," the possibility to take more time within the boundaries of the rules or simply to remain inactive, Reneman and Stronks, "What Are They Waiting For?" pp. 319–25.

[54] Griffiths, "Out of Time," p. 1999.

possibility to claim an effective legal remedy against the expulsion decision. For this reason, the ECtHR held

> [w]hile the urgent proceedings could in theory have been an opportunity for the court to examine the applicant's arguments and, if necessary, to stay the execution of the removal order, any possibility of that actually happening was extinguished because of the excessively short time between his application to the court and the execution of the removal order. In fact, the urgent-applications judge was powerless to do anything but declare the application devoid of purpose. So, the applicant was deported solely on the basis of the decision of the administrative authority. Consequently, in the circumstances of the present case the Court considers that the haste with which the removal order was executed had the effect of rendering the available remedies ineffective in practice and therefore inaccessible. While the Court is aware of the importance of swift access to a remedy, speed should not go so far as to constitute an obstacle or unjustified hindrance to making use of it, or take priority over its practical effectiveness.[55]

Extremely short procedures, in other words, can, just as excessively long procedures, serve as an obstruction to effective access to legal remedies. The relationship between time and power that Bourdieu puts to the fore in the figure of waiting, which indeed should be complemented with techniques of acceleration and haste, can, as we have just seen in the case of De Souze Ribeiro, be pinpointed in legal doctrine in the tenet of effective remedy and access to justice. I will return to this issue in Chapter 3 when I further discuss "waiting time."

Conclusion: Is There No End to the Manipulability of Time in Law?

Manipulation means, according to the Merriam-Webster dictionary, both to manage or utilize skilfully *and* to play unfairly or insidiously to one's own advantage. Etymologically, it stems from the Latin word *manus*, which means "hand." Manipulation could thus be defined as putting a situation to one's hand (as a Dutch saying has it) to utilize skillfully, no matter to what purpose. In other words, to grasp time in order to make it work for a certain policy aim. We have seen from the examples in this chapter that in migration law time is certainly skillfully used. The focus on the functioning of time in migration law revealed a multitude of possibilities to differentiate, categorize, and calculate human life by means of time. We have seen the intricate play between two complementing *and* contradicting forms of time: human time and clock time.

The success of clock time in law can be related to its objective character, which allows for quantification and calculation. It is this quantification that provides a clarity and logic to processes that are otherwise rather intangible. Since these processes happen in time, they can be referred to in clock time, whilst this reference obviously is based on an abstraction. It is precisely because clock time transforms what it supposedly measures that it is so successful: it is the transformation from an individual process of human time into quantifiable, calculable chunks of clock time that enables the simple, general application in law. An extra value of this generality is its visibility, it is easy to demonstrate that a certain policy has changed based on clock time. If one changes the period for naturalization from five to seven years, it becomes immediately apparent that it has become more difficult for migrants to

[55] ECHR December 13, 2012, *De Souza Ribeiro* v. *France*, 22689/07, paragraph 95.

become a national. With a simple change of terms, the policy change can be made visible and understandable.

However, legal time cannot be equated with clock time, the reference to time in law is always the time of someone, and therefore it is characterized by temporality. This temporality can be seen in every legal decision that creates a present, with a fixed past and a prospected future. The most obvious example of this role of human time in migration law is the categorization of certain forms of residence as "temporary" and others as "nontemporary" or "permanent." This implies a qualification of the future of the migrant at a certain moment, a qualification that always risks becoming outdated in the very future of that migrant.

We have witnessed the interplay of human time and clock time in several temporal differentiations that are at work in migration law: differentiation based on temporality, deadlines, qualification of time, antedating, and procedural differentiation. All of these forms of temporal governance have their own rationale and use the interplay between clock time and human time differently. Differentiations based on temporality seem to focus solely on human time, they fixate a categorization of different types of mobility on the moment of the decision about the residence permit. At that moment, they fix the past and the future in order to come to a legal decision. Hence, temporality can be used to qualify the enduring presence within a territory by qualifying it as either temporary or permanent residence. The case of the Ghanaian mother with which this book commenced puts this sort of differentiation to its extreme by raising the question of how long such temporary residence can endure. The locus of this sorts of differentiation is therefore the process of presence within a certain territory. It is this process that is being qualified as being temporary, and since this qualification is prospective, only residence that endures can legally be qualified as temporary. Residence that has been temporary, either because the migrant has left the territory or because the residence has become permanent, has not much legal value nor meaning. Yet, temporality can also be used to differentiate between sorts of behavior, as has been exemplified by the discussion of the "actual danger" criterion within the case-law of the CJEU in public order cases. In such cases, the pivotal question is whether it is likely that the migrant will in the same way in the future. This requires an analysis of the question of whether such a "propensity" can be witnessed in the migrant at the moment of the legal decision. Therefore, the evaluation of their behavior since the criminal offense is crucial for the question of whether there still exists such an actual danger. Temporality is used to make an estimation of the future on the basis of the behavior of the migrant in the (recent) past. Crucial to the usage of temporality is the fixation of a legally relevant moment on which the past and future are being evaluated. As we will see in the following chapters, such fixation can be observed not to relate well to lapse of time, or to the problem of extension, to put it more philosophically.

Deadlines and procedural differentiations, on the other hand, honor clock time, they use the calendar to attach certain legal consequences to moments on the calendar. Of course, human time is presumed, it is not just that after six months of clock time alien detention becomes (generally) unlawful, it is six months of the time of the specific migrant. Again, the process of presence within the territory is being used to differentiate. Countdown deadlines stipulate that after a certain period of time, a legal effect occurs, and because of their generality, they can be repeated. It is precisely in this repetitive character that the difference between clock and human time comes to the fore, as we will further discuss in the next chapter. Often countdown deadlines are accompanied by a form of qualification, almost never mere lapse of human time qualifies for a certain legal effect to occur, it will imply sorts of qualified time (lawful, uninterrupted, married, not precarious, nontemporary). In the qualification of time, differentiation is made in the presence of migrants over time by distinguishing between allowed and unwanted sorts of presence. In the qualification of time, human time and clock time firmly work together, for it is not about the mere ticking of the clock but about what happened in the life of the migrant as time went by. Next to countdown deadlines we have seen examples of recurrent deadlines (countdown deadlines that repeat themselves) and single-moment deadlines.

All of these forms of differentiation exemplify the ability to skillfully utilize time for the control of the enduring presence of migrants in a certain territory. The crucial question this book sets itself to answer is, however, precisely *when* this skillful management of time insidiously turns into unjust manipulation. Instead of focussing on the virtues of time, in the next chapter, I highlight the vices of time in law. Based on the work of philosophers such as Henri Bergson and Martin Heidegger, I will introduce three interrelated problems for the use of time in law. The problem of extension or lapse of time, the formal/material problem, and the finitude of human time.

2

The Vices of Legal Time

> A voice that is not yet ended, cannot be measured, so that it may be said how long, or short it is; nor can it be called equal to another, or double to a single, or the like. But when ended, it no longer is. How may it then be measured.
>
> Augustine, *Confessions*, 397 AD

> When the father creator saw the creature which he had made moving and living, the created image of the eternal gods, he rejoiced, and in his joy determined to make the copy still more like the original; and as this was eternal, he sought to make the universe eternal, so far as might be. Now the nature of the ideal being was everlasting, but to bestow this attribute in its fulness upon a creature was impossible. Wherefore he resolved to have a moving image of eternity, and when he set in order the heaven, he made this image eternal but moving according to number, while eternity itself rests in unity; and this image we call time.
>
> Plato, *Timaeus*, 360 BC

The possibilities of time as a means of control in law can hardly be overestimated. In the previous chapter, I focussed on the virtues of time – both clock and human time – to regulate and categorize the presence of migrants on a certain territory. Legal time makes use of a combination of both human and clock time and by means of temporal differentiations makes distinctions. Its success lies in the usage of the general, endless, and objective form of clock time, while constantly referring to the time of human beings, which is per definition individual, finite, and subjective. Moreover, it seems as if legal time does for temporal governance in migration law precisely what it promises: disciplining and controlling the presence of migrants on a territory by means of time.

In this chapter, however, I focus on the slithering character of legal time, the aspects of time that seem to slip through the grasping fingers of legal time. I analyze two temporal conundrums that partially overlap but have their own rationale: the formal/material divide; and the contrast between eternal and finite time.[1] It becomes apparent that these problems relate to the question of how to deal with lapse of time. In order to better appreciate the complexity of the latter issue, I will first introduce the problem of extension that is indeed related to both of the other problems.

The aim of these deliberations is to draw attention to the slippery character of human time; to emphasize that even though human time and clock time work together in legal

[1] This does not serve to say that these are the only legal problems that arise out of the problem of extension of time, there is a plenitude and a growing body of literature discussing them, see e.g. Chowdhury, *Time, Temporality and Legal Judgment*; E. Grabham and S. Beynon-Jones, eds., *Law and Time* (London: Routledge, 2020); Ranchordás and Roznai, *Time, Law and Change.*

time, in the end the two are fundamentally different. In the next chapter, I argue that the peculiar character of human time has normative value and that this risks being forgotten in the usage of legal time. In this chapter, however, the three discussions of time are particularly meant to argue that this necessarily leads to problems in migration law. In fact, the examples will time and again illustrate that these riddles can be resolved in law, albeit only for the time being. The underlying issues, however, rather reflect the aporias of human time.

Bergson and the Problem of Extension or the Reference to Processes

How can one measure the length of something that is still ongoing, this is the puzzling question that Augustine addresses in the quotation at the beginning of this chapter; how can one measure a voice that is still singing? As off topic as this question might seem, I would argue that this problem haunts every legal decision and every temporal differentiation. We have already seen it at work when discussing the example of the Eritrean girl in the introduction of the previous chapter, and also when discussing the question of whether a temporary migrant can reside long term, such as the example of the Ghanaian woman with whom I commenced this book. In both cases, the legal decision had to be made about a process that was still unfolding – even during the same procedure, such as the case of the Eritrean girl. So far, I have deliberately neglected this problem of lapse of time in order to highlight the successes of legal time. Yet, what is this problem exactly and why is it so challenging for the rigor of legal time?

In the following, I introduce the issue from the perspective of the philosophy of Henri Bergson and his appreciation of the experience of time. He argues that what is ordinarily understood as time is based on an overly mechanistic and scientific view generated by strict rationality, heavily leaning on mathematics. In his work, Bergson focussed instead on areas such as irrationality, becoming, memory, and intuitions – fields of inquiry that are indeed notoriously difficult to pin down. His philosophy can be seen as a countertendency to Enlightenment thinking that included Sade, Schopenhauer, and Nietzsche, but also a contemporary of Immanuel Kant, Moses Mendelssohn.[2] The experience of time is the key to understanding the approach that Bergson wishes to advance. His analysis of time has been of great influence on other modern critiques of time, such as critique of Husserl, Heidegger, and Levinas.

> [L]anguage requires us to establish between our ideas the same sharp and precise distinctions, the same discontinuity, as between material objects. This assimilation of thought to things is useful in practical life and necessary in most of the sciences. But it may be asked whether the insurmountable difficulties presented by certain philosophical problems do not arise from our placing side by side in space phenomena which do not occupy space, and whether, by merely getting rid of the clumsy symbols round which we are fighting, we might not bring the fight to an end.[3]

With these words, Henri Bergson commences his dissertation *Essai sur les données immédiates de la conscience* (1889), published in English as *Time and Free Will* (1910). In

[2] Hassan, *Empires of Speed*, p. 43. See for an astute analysis of time and rights in the light of the work of Moses Mendelssohn, Honig, *Emergency Politics*, pp. 40–64.

[3] Bergson, *Time and Free Will*, p. xix.

Time and Free Will, Bergson argues that our common conception of time is in fact "nothing but the ghost of space haunting the reflective consciousness."[4] Next to this conception, Bergson puts forward an understanding of time that is not governed by space, which he calls *durée*. His analysis of time will set the stage for my scrutiny of the pitfalls of legal time in migration law since many of the successes of legal time that we have encountered so far might also have arisen from a simplification of time, or the equation of time with space, to frame it in Bergson's terms.

Bergson contends that the common understanding of time is implicitly based on a conception of space because we imagine time as a series of points stretched out in space. This is the homogenous conception of time that I referred to in the introduction. We think of a moment (now) that is *preceded* by another moment, while *after* this particular moment another moment readily arrives. That in itself might not be too surprising a thought, the crux for Bergson is that this implies the simultaneous perception of these moments: we perceive them in a line and we see this line at once. This line is a continuity, it is a chain, the parts of which touch without penetrating one another. Bergson stresses, however, that we can only think of such an order when we first distinguish between the terms and then compare the places that they occupy, "hence we must perceive them as multiple, simultaneous and distinct."[5] Bergson's challenging insight is that by making such distinctions to create an order of succession, we imply the representation of time in space. Legal time bears witness to such an understanding of time, not only in the use of clock time but just as well in its usage of temporality. After all, the legally relevant moment of the legal decision presumes a before and after that can be related to one another in a certain continuum. At that moment, the relevant past and future must be made present to enable the legal assessment on which the decision is based. Nonetheless, how exactly is such an understanding of time spatial?

To understand how time is perceived as spatial and how Bergson distinguishes between two perceptions of time, the following example probably works best. Imagine a straight line of unlimited length and on this line a moving point. "If this point would be conscious of itself, it would feel itself change, since it moves: it would perceive a succession; but would this succession assume for it the form of a line?"[6] Bergson stresses that it would be possible to see the succession in the form of a line, yet for this, the point should rise above the line to perceive it as such. Therefore, the different positions should be perceived at once simultaneously in juxtaposition. To perceive it as a line, it would be necessary to take a position outside it, to take account of the void that surrounds it and think of it in spatial terms. Such a perspective presumes a fixation of the stream of time on a specific moment in which the spectator oversees the stream. It is not difficult to see the parallel with a legal judgment that must be made at a particular moment, and consequently fixating the ever-flowing stream of life in a past, present, and future. In a legal decision, the life of the applicant is situated on a line which presumes the moment on which the legal decision is taken. Relevant events of their life can be related to one another by putting them in a temporal order, in which events precede and follow one another. By these means, the legal decision necessarily implies an external position to the experienced individual time. That in itself might not be a surprising conclusion, what Bergson describes is, after all, a subjective stance; he endeavors to describe the experience of one's own time. The moment someone else judges my time, this already

[4] Ibid., p. 100. [5] Ibid., p. 102. [6] Ibid., p. 103.

presumes an externalization, the distanced perspective of someone else's time. Again, disguising as measurement, the clock transforms what it seeks to refer to, as Hassan puts it.

Then what is this qualitative difference between the experience of time and the measurement of time with the clock? It is this difference that will be crucial for a good understanding of the shortcomings of legal time. It is clear that Bergson is not satisfied with clock time, which he does not dismiss but sees as just one perception of time. He tries to find alongside this homogenous conception of time – a conception of time that is characterized by simultaneous, distinguishable points stretched out as a line – a heterogeneous conception of time. Such "pure duration" would be the form in which the succession of our conscious states is not separated into distinguishable, spatial mental states. It is rather in a "stream of consciousness," as William James describes, that we live. Without the outsider's perspective, without a perspective that transcends it, the point will not perceive itself as moving linearly. "Its sensations will add themselves dynamically to one another and will organize themselves, like the successive notes of a tune by which we allow ourselves to be lulled and soothed."[7] This is what Bergson calls "duration," being "nothing but a succession of qualitative changes, which melt into and permeate one another, without precise outlines, without any tendency to externalize themselves in relationship to one another."[8] Only when we start to divide this stream into singular moments do we secretly bring space into the equation. "[I]t is enough that, in recalling these [mental] states, it does not set them alongside its actual state as one point alongside another, but forms both the past and the present states into an organic whole, as happens when we recall the notes of a tune, melting, so to speak, into one another."[9]

Bergson's reference to music in this quotation is no coincidence: the understanding of time that grasps the movement of it is often related to rhythm and music.[10] It is only with the musical metaphor that Bergson can clearly illustrate what he seeks.

> Might it not be said that, even if these notes succeed one another, yet we perceive them in one another, and that their totality may be compared to a living being whose parts, although distinct, permeate one another just because they are so closely connected? The proof is that, if we interrupt the rhythm by dwelling longer than is right on one note of the tune, it is not its exaggerated length, as length, which will warn us of our mistake, but the qualitative change thereby caused in the whole of the musical phrase. We can thus conceive of succession without distinction, and think of it as a mutual penetration, an inter-connexion and organization of elements, each one of which represents the whole, and cannot be distinguished or isolated from it except by abstract thought.[11]

The tones of music mutually penetrate each other and thus cannot be distinguished because they are part of the melody. In a "stream of consciousness," the mental states or images of

[7] Ibid., p. 186. [8] Ibid., p. 104. [9] Ibid., p. 100.

[10] See Augustine, *Confessions*, trans. H. Chadwick (Oxford: Oxford University Press, 2009), chapter 11, he discusses the duration of a sound. In F. Nietzsche, *De Geboorte van de Tragedie of Griekse Cultuur en Pessimisme*, trans. H. Driessen (Amsterdam: De Arbeiderspers, 2009), Nietzsche does so by his duality of the Appolinian and Dyonisian. A. Schopenhauer, *Die Welt Als Wille und Vorstellung* (Munich: Deutscher Taschenbuch Verlag GmbH & Co., 1998), sees music as the highest form of understanding. Bergson illustrates his durée often with reference to music or the sound of a clock, and more recently, H. Rosa, *Resonanz: Eine Soziologie der Weltbeziehung* (Frankfurt: Suhrkamp Verlag GmbH, 2016).

[11] Bergson, *Time and Free Will*, pp. 100–1.

reality permeate each other, spill over, and provide a streaming impression of reality that is at odds with the spatialized conception that is presumed in our punctual understanding of time.

To understand the difference between the two conceptions of time, and to see how this distinction is at work in legal time, it is crucial to see the conceptual difference in exteriority and succession. Both are central to Bergson but were already to Augustine of Hippo (354–80), a millennium and a half earlier. The point is, as Augustine puts forward, we measure time from the instant it began, until the end it left. "For we measure the time interval itself from some beginning point to some end."[12] So take for example, again, a sound; how could we measure it?, asks Augustine. The point is that we can measure from the instant something has started to the instant it has ended, yet the paradox is that a voice that is not yet ended cannot be measured but when ended, it no longer is. An instant has no presence, since it immediately ceases to exist. The possibility to divide the instant into smaller portions is endless and we will not find a solid ground of presence.[13] "And yet we measure times," Augustine argues, "not those which are not yet, nor those which no longer are, northose which are stretched out by some delay, nor those which have no limit. Therefore, we measure neither times future nor times past, nor times present, nor times passing by; and yet we do measure times."[14]

This is what Bergson means when he says that when focussing on moments, there is immediately a certain exteriority. However, because of this spatialization, there is no succession, there is only the "now" in which we perceive this particular moment, as it is distinguished from earlier and later moments. As we have seen in the example of the conscious point on the line, if the point perceives itself on a line, it must take a position in which the points are perceived at once. This implies that there is no succession. Every position of the point on the line implies a new perception of all of the spatial positions, the precise position of the point itself and the line on which all of the positions relate to each other. Movement and succession are necessarily excluded in such an exterior, fixating view.

In our stream of consciousness, on the other hand, there is succession, since the mental states permeate each other in a constant indistinguishable flow. This implies a constant movement, yet there is no exteriority in such a stream. Only if we distinguish, do we bring a division between certain states and therewith space and exteriority. "We can thus conceive of succession without distinction, and think of it as a mutual penetration, an interconnexion and organization of elements, each one of which represents the whole, and cannot be distinguished or isolated from it except by abstract thought."[15]

The question of lapse of time can accordingly be approached from two mutually excluding perspectives: a streaming flow of qualitative changes that constantly permeate one another; or the exterior perspective of moments that can be distinguished as a line. The former time, which Bergson calls *durée*, is the experience of time, whilst the latter shares characteristics with what we have so far called clock time. To be sure, this duration is not

[12] Augustine, *Confessions*, trans. Outler, book XI, chapter XXVII, par. 34 (or pagenumber 201).

[13] This problem was already put forward by Aristotle, "But of time, though it is divisible, some parts have been, some parts are to come, but no part is. The now is not a part," Physics IV, 218a 3–8, see for an extensive discussion of Aristotle's conception of time, U. Coope, *Time for Aristotle*, Oxford Aristotle Studies (Oxford: Oxford University Press, 2008).

[14] Augustine, *Confessions*, trans. Outler, book XI, chapter XXVII, par. 34 (or pagenumber 201).

[15] Bergson, *Time and Free Will*, p. 101.

the same as what we have so far called human time. After all, the problems Bergson puts to the fore equally apply to the conception of human time. The temporality of human time that distinguishes between a past, present, and future just as well implies a certain exteriority from the successive flow of qualitative changes that Bergson identifies as the experience of time.

Yet, with this analysis of Bergson in mind, we can now more accurately pinpoint the success of legal time, which is based on the use of both clock time and human time, as seen in the previous chapter. The success of legal time is to be found in its exterior character. It is the exterior perspective that enables distinctions between points in the past, present, and future. And as soon as we have rewritten the time of the migrant on a given territory as constituting a line, we can start using deadlines and start making temporal differentiations. A countdown deadline is after all only conceivable if one first relates the life of the migrant to the timeline of the deadline, for example, by starting the clock upon arrival of the migrant in the territory and stopping it five years later. Moreover, clearly a differentiation between temporary and permanent migrants is based on the fixation of the timeline of the migrant at a certain moment. In both cases, the temporal differentiation is based on an exterior perspective that freezes the processes to which it, nevertheless, refers. The latter clearly being one of the advantages of legal time: the ability to refer to processes that happen in time that would otherwise be hard to put into words, let alone into clear material criteria.

So, why then is this a legal problem? After all, with Elizabeth Cohen, I have earlier presented this capacity of clock time as a solution, rather than a problem. Bergson might be right that the homogenous conception of time is categorically different from the experience of time; but if this is so indescribable and indistinguishable as he suggests, then the question arises of whether there is room for such a heterogenous conception of time in law. I would argue, however, that we should not strive so much for the further inclusion of Bergson's *durée* in legal time.[16] Indeed, his analysis points toward the fundamental inadequacy or instability of every reference to processes. The clock might be praised for its reference to processes that happen in time but we should also be very careful: the reference always risks missing the point. The succession of human time is, in the end, categorically different from the exterior reference to it. It is against the background of this fundamental question of extension that we arrive at two persistent problems of legal time: the formal/material problem; and eternal *versus* finite time. The reference to processes in law is not only problematic and complex, a pure exterior reference to human time misses the most fundamental aspect of it: its mortality. To be sure, the aim of this chapter is not to argue that these two problems of time necessarily lead to great difficulties in the usage of legal time. The point is merely to stress the vice of legal time – as in the incompleteness or deficiency – in its reference to human time, by bringing frontward the peculiar characteristics of human time and the difficulties of any reference to it. In the next chapter, I argue that these deficiencies of legal time can turn into vices in the moral sense, if the normative value of human time risks being trapped in grasping, temporal, legal control.

[16] For a more detailed analysis of Bergson's conception of time and its relevance to law, see A. Lefebvre, *The Image of Law* (Stanford, CA: Stanford University Press, 2008); A. Lefebvre, "Human Rights in Deleuze and Bergson's Later Philosophy," in *Deleuze and Law*, eds. L. de Sutter and K. McGee (Edinburgh: Edinburgh University Press, 2012), pp. 48–68.

General or Unique Time: The Formal/Material Problem

The first problem can best be described when focussing on long-term residing or settled migrants and their claims for inclusion.[17] In such cases, there is an intricate relationship between the usage of time in law and their reference to the processes of migrants living on a certain territory. Long-term residing migrants can claim stronger residence entitlements or apply for naturalization, at least European migration law bears witness to this starting point. In debates about citizenship, this is also a widely shared assumption. Shachar, for example, refers to US court decisions that put forward the argument that stronger ties and affiliation are presumed to have grown over time for lawfully residing long-term residents. If the principle is at work in law regulating the status of lawfully residing migrants, it must apply to irregular migrants, Shachar argues. Furthermore, she refers to the work of Motomura and stresses that rootedness is an "incremental process in which one's centre of life-gravity shifts."[18] After a lapse of time, one's center of life gradually changes – the longer one resides, the more the center of one's life will be at the place of habitual residence. Joseph Carens has a similar stance on this issue, "most people," Carens stresses "form their deepest human connections where they live – it becomes home."[19] Also, marriage creates deep ties and living with one's family over time creates deep ties with the place where one lives. Moreover, "[w]e sink deep roots over [time],"[20] holds Carens. He defends the inclusion of long-term residing migrants as part of his theory of "social membership."[21]

We sink deep roots over time, is clearly the crux of the matter; the process of becoming rooted in a place is situated in time. And becoming rooted can become an argument for the inclusion of the migrant as a member of the community. Nonetheless, how can this process of rootedness be operationalized in legal terms? In European law, one can discern two approaches to this question, but in the end, both manage to miss the point.

Time as Proxy

The first approach is to be found in the earlier mentioned European Union (EU) Long-Term Residence Directive. The assumption about rootedness is also central to this Directive. As early as the Tampere meeting of the European Council in 1999, the suggestion was made that the legal status of third-country nationals should be approximated to that of Member State nationals. The Council declared that a person who has resided legally in a Member State for a significant period of time and who holds a long-term residence permit should be granted a set of uniform rights in that Member State that are as near as possible to those enjoyed by citizens of the EU. The Long-Term Residence Directive is the result of this promise. Its clear objective is to provide stronger rights to those third-country nationals

[17] In literature, long-term migrants are also referred to as "denizens," stressing their liminal position between the category of aliens and full-blown citizens, see e.g. T. Hammar, "Legal Time of Residence and the Status of Immigrants," in *From Aliens to Citizens: Redefining the Status of Immigrants in Europe*, ed. R. Bauböck (Vienna: European Centre, 1994).

[18] A. Shachar, "Earned Citizenship: Property Lessons for Immigration Reform," *Yale Journal of Law and the Humanities* 23, no. 1 (2011), p. 131.

[19] J. H. Carens, *Immigrants and the Right to Stay* (Cambridge, MA: The MIT Press, 2010), p. 12.

[20] Ibid., p. 17.

[21] J. H. Carens, *The Ethics of Immigration* (Oxford: Oxford University Press, 2013), chapter 8.

who reside a significant period of time in the territory.[22] It is clear from the outset that the duration of residence is the most important criterion for the acquisition of a long-term residence status. This is also stipulated in Recital 6, which states that

> [t]he main criterion for acquiring the status of long-term resident should be the duration of residence in the territory of a Member State. Residence should be both legal and continuous in order to show that the person has put down roots in the country. Provision should be made for a degree of flexibility so that account can be taken of circumstances in which a person might have to leave the territory on a temporary basis.[23]

Correspondingly, the European Court of Human Rights (ECtHR) has stressed on several occasions that it is precisely the relationship between time and ties that Article 8 of the European Convention on Human Rights (ECHR) protects. It stipulated that Article 8 also protects the right to establish and develop relationships "with other human beings and the outside world," and this implies that the social ties between settled migrants and their community are protected under this provision.[24] In a series of pivotal cases, the Court has stipulated that criteria must be taken into account when deciding whether a residence permit of a settled migrant can be withdrawn without breaching Article 8.[25] One important criterion for an analysis focussing on the time spent on the territory by the migrant is "the solidity of social, cultural and family ties with the host country and with the country of destination." The Court formulated this criterion for the first time explicitly in the case of *Üner*. In fact, the Court linked it to the time criterion put forward earlier in the *Boultif* case:

> Indeed, the rationale behind making the duration of a person's stay in the host country one of the elements to be taken into account lies in the assumption that the longer a person has been residing in a particular country, the stronger his or her ties with that country and the weaker the ties with the country of his or her nationality will be.[26]

This formulation of the Court is reminiscent of the recital of the Long-Term Residence Directive, which stated that residence must be "legal and continuous in order to show that the person has put down roots in the country."

Clearly, both legal instruments attempt to catch the process of the migrant becoming rooted in a given territory, or to put it in terms of Bergson, these are attempts to incorporate the succession of temporal experiences of the migrant in a given territory. As such, the examples from the case-law of Article 8 and the EU Long-Term Residence Directive are paradigmatic for the debate on the inclusion of long-term residing migrants since they overlap with scholarly discussions on ius nexi and ius domicili. It can be observed, however, that both refer to the process from an exterior position and both attempts fail to grasp the experience of time, albeit in different ways. It is therefore worthwhile scrutinizing the exact connection with time in the different approaches.

The similarity between the Long-Term Residence Directive and the case-law of Article 8 is that time is taken as a proxy for something else that apparently changes over

[22] Recital 2, Long-Term Residence Directive (Directive 2003/109).

[23] This is reiterated in CJEU July 17, 2014, *Tahir*, C-469/13, paragraph 30: "[the] residence requirement is an essential condition for the grant of long-term resident status."

[24] ECHR October 18, 2006, *Üner* v. *the Netherlands*, 46410/99, paragraph 59.

[25] ECHR November 2, 2001, *Boultif* v. *Switzerland*, 54273/00; ECHR October 18, 2006, *Üner* v. *the Netherlands*, 46410/99; ECHR June 23, 2008, *Maslov* v. *Austria*, 1638/03.

[26] ECHR October 18, 2006, *Üner* v. *the Netherlands*, 46410/99, paragraph 58.

time. Migrants grow deeper roots over time and they will have stronger ties with their country of residence, at least that is the assumption. Joseph Carens has explicitly defended this usage of time as proxy, "residence and time are proxies for richer, deeper forms of connection but that we have both practical and principled reasons not to try to go beyond these proxies, at least under most circumstances."[27] Just like Cohen, he praises the usage of clock time for its objective character and its ability to refer to processes that are otherwise difficult to grasp. Yet, Carens accepts that this is an assumption and might not apply for everyone. "*Most* people do develop deep and rich networks of relationships in the place where they live, and this normal pattern of human life is what makes sense of the idea of social membership."[28]

Meanwhile, it is important to see the precise correlation between time and ties. In fact, time is qualified by relating it to ties. It is not mere lapse of time that plays a role in the assessment of the ECtHR, it is "one of the criteria," and moreover, it is only assumed that the migrant gains stronger ties over lapse of time with the country. This is vital for understanding Article 8: with the passing of time, it is assumed that the migrant has ties with the country, and yet, this remains to be proven.

Here we see a crucial difference between time in the Long-Term Residence Directive and time under Article 8. Under the former, it is assumed that over time migrants in general grow deep roots in the country, after the lapse of five years this assumption is enough for stronger entitlements for every individual (as long as the time is continuous and lawful). Such an understanding of time resonates Carens argument for the usage of residence and time as proxy for social membership. The case-law of Article 8 might commence from the same assumption that ties grow over time, it does not use a clock time criterion to put this into practice. In Article 8, the assumption of time must further be substantiated; it must be argued that the migrant indeed has strong ties with the country. This proves that time under Article 8 has an individual signification (the alleged ties that grow over time must be substantiated in every individual case), while time under the Long-Term Residence Directive has a general meaning (the general assumption is enough for every individual).

Individual, Material Time

What does such an individual substantiation imply? Time under Article 8 is individualized by an actual assessment of the ties of the migrants with both the host country and the

27 Carens, *The Ethics of Immigration*, p. 165.

28 Ibid., p. 168. Sarah Song has criticized Carens's precisely on this point, since the boundaries of affiliations "do not map neatly onto territorial boundaries" and it does not provide a strong argument for short-term and temporary visitors; S. Song, "The Significance of Territorial Presence and the Rights of Immigrants," in *Migration in Political Theory* (Oxford: Oxford University Press, 2016), pp. 230–1. Sarah van Walsum has equally argued that ties are in cases of family migration transnational, therewith complicating the classic Westphalian understanding of the relationship between territory and affiliation; S. K. van Walsum, *The Family and the Nation: Dutch Family Migration Policies in the Context of Changing Family Norms* (Newcastle upon Tyne: Cambridge Scholars Publishing, 2008); S. K. van Walsum, *Intimate Strangers*, Migration Law Series (Amsterdam: Vrije Universiteit Amsterdam, 2012). Paulina Ochoa Espejo has criticized presence-based arguments for inclusion such as ius nexi and ius temporis for silently grounding a right in something else, namely, connection's to the state's society, see P. Ochoa Espejo, "Taking Place Seriously: Territorial Presence and the Rights of Immigrants," *The Journal of Political Philosophy* 24, no. 1 (2016), pp. 67–87.

country of origin. All of the circumstances of the case must be assessed. The question of whether they speak the language of the host country[29] is relevant as well as the language of the country of origin,[30] whether they have work,[31] took primary education[32] or studied,[33] or that they are a member of a church community[34] are all important circumstances. Interestingly enough, the material assessment of the ties is often also expressed merely in terms of time: the length of the period of residence in the country;[35] the length of residence in the country of origin;[36] the number of times they went back to their country of origin;[37] the age at which the migrant came to the country;[38] whether the residence forms a "considerable length of time in a person's life";[39] whether the migrant is still of an "adaptable age";[40] and where they spent their "formative years."[41]

Also, the family ties are often expressed in terms of time. An important indication for the effectiveness of the marriage is for example the length of it.[42] Similarly important is the question of whether there are any children of the marriage, and if so, their age.[43] As to the relation between parent and children, whether the migrant has a caring role and the children are dependent on them[44] and whether they actually live together is pertinent.[45] If the child is an adult, it is important whether they have founded a family themselves.[46] For the children, many of the aforementioned aspects are relevant: What age did they arrive in the country? Did they spend their formative years there? How long have they lived in the country of origin of the parent and how often have they been to the country of origin of the parent? Did they enjoy education? Do they speak the language (both of the host country and the country of origin of the parent)? and do they have the nationality of the host country?[47]

We take from this brief overview of relevant criteria in the balancing under Article 8 that a description of the ties that have developed after a lapse of time is endless. The same goes for what Ayelet Shachar argues in her pledge for a jus nexi. Shachar has proposed "a new theoretical framework that emphasizes the importance of rootedness as a basis for a legal title."[48] She argues that "jus nexi reflects the idea of democratic inclusion, according to

[29] See ECHR December 4, 2012, *Butt* v. *Norway*, 47017/09, paragraph 58.
[30] See ECHR January 8, 2009, *Joseph Grant* v. *the United Kingdom*, 10606/07, paragraph 41.
[31] See ECHR October 9, 2003, *Slivenko* v. *Austria*, 48321/99, paragraph 123.
[32] See ECHR June 23, 2008, *Maslov* v. *Austria*, 1638/03, paragraph 96.
[33] See ECHR September 20, 2011, *A. A.* v. *the United Kingdom*, 8000/08, paragraph 66.
[34] Ibid., paragraph 64.
[35] See ECHR December 9, 2010, *Gezginci* v. *Switzerland*, 16372/05, paragraphs 69–70.
[36] See ECHR February 19, 1998, *Dahlia* v. *France*, 154/1996/773/974, paragraph 53.
[37] See ECHR February 17, 2009, *Onur* v. *the United Kingdom*, 27319/07, paragraph 57.
[38] See ECHR June 14, 2011, *Osman* v. *Denmark*, 38058/09, paragraph 68.
[39] See ECHR April 16, 2013, *Udeh* v. *Switzerland*, 12020/09, paragraph 48.
[40] See ECHR June 22, 1999, *Ajayi* v. *the United Kingdom*, 27663/95 (decision).
[41] See ECHR November 24, 2009, *Omojudi* v. *the United Kingdom*, 1820/08, paragraph 45.
[42] See ECHR March 26, 1992, *Beldjoudi* v. *France*, 12083/86, paragraph 76; ECHR November 2, 2001, *Boultif* v. *Switzerland*, 54273/00, paragraph 48.
[43] See ECHR November 2, 2001, *Boultif* v. *Switzerland*, 54273/00, paragraph 48.
[44] See ECHR January 8, 2009, *Joseph Grant* v. *the United Kingdom*, 10606/07, paragraph 40.
[45] See ECHR February 17, 2009, *Onur* v. *the United Kingdom*, 27319/07, paragraph 58.
[46] See ECHR September 23, 2010, *Bousarra* v. *France*, 25672/07, paragraphs 38–9.
[47] See ECHR December 20, 2011, *A. H. Khan* v. *the United Kingdom*, 6222/10, paragraph 39.
[48] Shachar, "Earned Citizenship," p. 113. The article seems to be an application of her theory as developed in the *Birthright Lottery* to the specific US debate on the regularization of unlawful migrants. An

which those who are habitually subject to the coercive powers of the state must gain a hand in shaping its laws, if they so choose."[49] Citing the *Nottebohm* case, she stresses that the social fact of attachment and the real and effective link between an individual and a nation are the basis for membership. Shachar immediately acknowledges the individual character of these criteria and the difference in weight and importance that should be attached to it, yet attempts to compile with a nonexhaustive list of factors, which she calls, quoting the *Nottebohm* case, the "center-of-interest test." Among these factors are: family ties; habitual residence; attachment shown to a given country and inculcated in any children; length of residence; evidence of value and service to the community; employment history; the extreme hardship that might be incurred by the respondent or their family if deportation was to take place; age; health; ability to travel; moral character; whether they volunteer on school boards; whether they contribute to the work of religious organizations; and so on. Shachar clearly tries to find material criteria to define rootedness and her findings are similar to those from the case-law on Article 8 ECHR.

Just as with this Court's case-law, the criteria are very case-based, individual, and indeed endless. Shachar seems to deliberately leave open the list of criteria that could prove the shifted center of interest. This, however, hints at a rather fundamental problem: the moment one starts to provide a material description of what happened with the migrant over time, any generality seems to fade away. Moreover, it becomes difficult to discern the precise relationship between these ties and time. Take again the case-law of the ECtHR. At first sight, it seems that time is expressed in terms of ties, yet often such ties are again articulated in terms of time. As we have seen in the previous discussion, the arguments just consist of descriptions of ties (education, work, language, etc.) or merely sum up elements of time (the moment one arrived, the length of residence, the length of marriage). Obviously, many arguments have both a meaning related to time and material meaning. "Formative years," education, language, work, and so on, gain particular weight by expressing their length in terms of time. Unfortunately, it remains fairly vague as to the material aspect (What is the precise relationship between the substance and time?) and the time aspect (When are these formative years precisely? How long do they last? How does it relate to the concept of "adaptable age," etc.?). Furthermore, if the relationship between time and ties already remains a puzzling question for an individual, it seems to be quite impossible to draw any general conclusions on the relationship on time and ties. The previous list of relevant ties does not lend itself for generalization, hence it remains unclear whether something general can be said about the relationship between time and ties.

General, Formal time

The opposite is true for the pure clock time criterion that we found at work in the Long-Term Residence Directive, but which is also at the heart of any jus domicilii reasoning in the scholarly debate. Bauböck, for example, argues in favor of inclusion based on domicile: citizenship would be acquired automatically after a short period of residence and also lost automatically when moving to another state.[50] A radical proponent of such a jus domicilii

important aspect of her analysis (in both the book and the article) is an analogy with property law, which, however interesting, I must leave aside.

49 Ibid., p. 179. 50 Bauböck, "Temporary Migrants, Partial Citizenship and Hypermigration," p. 685.

principle has been Rubio-Marín, who has argued that after a certain time, resident migrants should automatically become citizens, without applying for naturalization, without having to renounce prior nationality, and irrespective of whether their initial residence status had been legal or illegal.[51]

Rubio-Marín writes

> [i]t follows that in the case of immigrants, their qualification as societal members does not correspond to any legally defined immigration status, but rather refers to the actual reality of people who migrate and come to live and work in a place in which they naturally develop a set of attachments and which, after a long residence period, they are likely to make the centre of their existence in practical terms.[52]

This likelihood is crucial in such a formal criterion; the link with the life of the migrant is assumed, as was also explicitly defended by Carens. It follows that in the most radical version of jus domicilii, the reference to the individual process of rootedness is lost. There is no test of whether the migrant has actually put down roots in the country, this is simply assumed. Certainly, this is precisely the advantage of a clock time criterion, as Cohen and Carens stress, referring to a process without pinpointing the exact relationship. And indeed, this element is clearly presented as an asset in a domicilii principle, it implies "the inclusion of all residents independent of arbitrary criteria."[53] Milder versions of jus domicilii might only allow for lawful residence and request naturalization instead of automatically becoming a citizen.

Yet, the crux of the matter is that under a jus domicilii principle, the usage of a clock time criterion means that the reference to the process in the individual case is lost. In any case, it will be impossible to establish in the individual instance whether there is *sufficient* rootedness.

Grasping the Process of Time

So, we encounter two attempts to catch the experience of lived time on a certain territory in a given period. We have the formal and general time of the Long-Term Residence Directive, and the material and individual time of the case-law of Article 8 ECHR, corresponding to the formal jus domicilii principle and the material jus nexi argument. Both suffer from a problem; both lose something in their reference, albeit different things. In the former, the specific individual circumstances of the case are lost, in the latter, any generality fades away. The five years of clock time refers to the process of rootedness, which indeed develops in time, without pinpointing the exact relationship with rootedness of the particular individual. This is what Shachar has called the problem of "overinclusion", the legal criterion includes more than it aims to include.[54] In a pure jus domicilii principle, as put forward by Rubio-Marín, the only important point would be mere lapse of time. If the time threshold is met, citizenship is

[51] Rubio-Marín, *Immigration as a Democratic Challenge*, p. 102. [52] Ibid., p. 22.

[53] H. Bauder, "Domicile Citizenship, Migration and the City," in *Migration Policy and Practice: Interventions and Solutions*, eds. H. Bauder and C. Matheis (New York: Palgrave, 2016), p. 91. Bauder argues that the jus domicilii principle should be accompanied with open borders, see also H. Bauder, "Jus Domicile: In Pursuit of a Citizenship of Equality and Social Justice," *Journal of International Political Theory* 8, nos. 1–2 (2012).

[54] Shachar, *The Birthright Lottery*.

automatically acquired without additional requirements. On the basis of a pure jus nexi principle, however, we would have a nonconclusive list of material criteria, yet ultimately this would imply that the link with time would have been lost. After all, it is fairly possible that one's "center-of-interest" is already linked to a certain territory *before* one arrives there, because of family ties or work, for example.[55] Just as it is perfectly conceivable that one's "center-of-interest" would *never* shift. After all, every material criterion that assesses the membership of a migrant excludes those who do not meet these criteria.[56]

Take, for example, the rather straightforward criterion of language, many will argue that ties to a certain place entail at least a certain mastery of the distinctive language.[57] In addition, let us assume that we can come to an agreement as to which particular proficiency of the language would testify to the required "rootedness." Even here, the relationship with lapse of time would be lost; an individual migrant could fullfil this criterion at any moment – after one year, possibly five years – but it is also perfectly conceivable that for some migrants it would take ten years or longer. Moreover, as integration research shows, it can be virtually impossible to reach certain language requirements for some illiterate migrants.[58] That said, some migrants might master the language already *before* entering the territory. A material time criterion that aims to grasp the rootedness of migrants who have lived on a certain territory over a period of time, therefore, risks overinclusion *and* under inclusion. Some migrants might be included without living on the territory, whilst others might live there without being included.

Accordingly, we have reached the following paradox: the attempts of both material and formal time criteria to grasp the experience of time are inept. Material time criteria are highly individual, they lack generality and therefore they cannot be related to a general period of clock time. Material criteria, in other words, presume exteriority, for they can be met at any moment; it is the external glance at the life of an individual at a particular moment that is tested via the material criteria. This implies, however, that with an assessment based on material criteria, one cannot assess succession; it is merely an assessment of a particular moment in the life of the migrant, no matter how that moment relates to the particular past or future of that moment, nor to the time spent on the territory. This is a problem because the material time criterion is intended to test the process in the first place. Formal criteria, on the other hand, have generality but lack the reference to the lived experiences of the individual migrant altogether. A formal time criterion, in other words, might relate to the time spent on the territory, but lacks reference to individual experiences.

[55] Van Walsum, *Intimate Strangers*.

[56] There is ample research about the exclusionary force of integration requirements, e.g. A. Böcker and T. Strik, "Language and Knowledge Tests for Permanent Residence Rights: Help or Hindrance for Integration?," *European Journal of Migration and Law* 13, no. 2 (2011); de Waal, "Conditional Belonging"; T. M. de Waal, *Integration Requirements for Immigrants in Europe: A Legal-Philosophical Inquiry* (London: Bloomsbury, 2021); E. Guild, C. A. Groenendijk, and S. Carrera, *Illiberal Liberal States* (Farnham: Ashgate, 2009); W. Schinkel, *Imagined Societies: A Critique of Immigrant Integration in Western Europe* (Cambridge: Cambridge University Press, 2017); R. van Oers, E. Ersboll, and D. Kostakopoulou, *A Re-definition of Belonging* (Leiden: Martinus Nijhoff, 2009).

[57] D. Miller, *Strangers in Our Midst: The Political Philosophy of Immigration* (Cambridge, MA: Harvard University Press, 2016), p. 132–4.

[58] Van Oers, Ersboll, and Kostakopoulou, *A Re-definition of Belonging*.

In migration law, one will often see both systems at work simultaneously (five years of residence plus an integration test). Nevertheless, it is important to note that if taken to its extreme (just clock time, just material criteria), they lose the reference to precisely the processes that these criteria aim to encapsulate. Also, importantly, as will appear in the next chapter, upon close scrutiny, this problem reveals an additional argument for the inclusion of migrants that is hidden behind the claims for jus nexi and jus domicilii: the argument of jus temporis. Whereas jus nexi and jus domicilii both have intrinsic argumentative force, they both fail to address the particular characteristics of human time. Consequently, it is precisely in the reference to the mere lapse of human time on a territory that one can find a further argument for the inclusion of migrants based on time.

Heidegger, Eternity, and Mortality

The second difficulty of legal time points out a rather crucial difference between time of the clock and time of human beings: the former is endless, whilst the latter is finite. This problem of time has most urgently been advanced by Martin Heidegger (1889–1976). Clearly influenced by the philosophy of Henri Bergson, he criticized Western philosophy for prioritizing the present as a linear series of now points. In this tradition of thought, "past" is called what is no longer *present*, and the future what is not yet *present*. This implies that temporality is understood from the perspective of the present, and it is presented as if this present is immovable. Indeed, as we have seen in the discussion of Bergson, such a perspective does not allow for succession, whilst it introduces exteriority. In other words, it is this very perspective that brings the streaming flow of time to a stop in the present moment. After all, it is in the present moment that one perceives the endless past and future moments. This conception of abstract time consists of an eternal sequence of nows, each now replaceable by the next moment. Therefore, the present moment can be seen as a moving image of eternity, as Plato describes in the epigraph at the beginning of this chapter. Severson has succinctly summarized this point "[t]his Platonic position takes its bearings from the fact that no matter how one divides up time it is always *now*. Now is always available, without interruption, as 'present-at-hand' (*vorhanden*)."[59] Eternity similarly presumes such an immovable form of time.

> Who shall hold it and fix it so that it may come to rest for a little; and then, by degrees, glimpse the glory of that eternity which abides forever; and then, comparing eternity with the temporal process in which nothing abides, they may see that they are incommensurable? They would see that a long time does not become long, except from the many separate events that occur in its passage, which cannot be simultaneous. In the Eternal, on the other hand, nothing passes away, but the whole is simultaneously present

asks Augustine in his *Confessions*.[60] From the viewpoint of the eternal, the whole is eternally present, there is neither past nor future. A conception of time that is grounded in the infinite sequence of present moments is a moving image of eternity, nothing passes away and the whole seems to be present at once.

59 E. Severson, *Levinas's Philosophy of Time* (Pittsburgh: Duquesne University Press, 2013), p. 13.
60 Augustine, *Confessions*, trans. Outler, book XI, chapter XI, par. 13 (or pagenumber 191).

Heidegger criticizes this understanding of time for being too rational and impersonal; instead, he proposes a radically different conceptualization of being in time. In thinking about time, one is always already thrown in a world as a temporal being – which Heidegger calls *Dasein*. The concept of time should not be sought outside of human existence, as it is the case when one sees time as an image of eternity; on the contrary, the concept of time is grounded in human existence. "Dasein is time, time is temporal. Dasein is not time, but temporality,"[61] Heidegger concludes in *The Concept of Time*, published in 1924, three years before his seminal work *Being and Time*.[62] Heidegger, in other words, puts the traditional conception of time on its head, the temporality of human time is the primordial form of time, clock time is always already an abstraction from a more primary experience of time. "*Time itself* is meaningless; time is temporal."[63] It is the existence of a human being that at every moment extends to the future and the past, humans are *zukünftig* (future-oriented/dependent) and *gewesen* (having been).[64]

Time for Heidegger, therefore, is not so much the image of eternity, as in the Platonic tradition of thought; rather, time finds its image in our finitude. Besides, this primordial conception of human time has a direction, from birth to death, and is characterized most by its finitude. As easy as it is to turn the clock back, it is impossible to turn back human time. It is important to observe the crucial difference with an eternal conception of time: "As time passes, so do our possibilities. The passing of time and indeed such restrictions are thus meaningful only for a being that lives with an understanding of a limit," as Alweiss stresses.[65] For Heidegger, it is only because human beings are defined by death and have the certainty of mortality that we have an understanding of the finitude of time.

For the purposes of this book, it is not really necessary to establish which conception of time is primary, if that would be possible at all,[66] but it is crucial to see the difference between these two conceptions of time in Heidegger's account. With Bergson, we could identify the distinction between a streaming conception of time and a fixed understanding of it. Heidegger adds to this that the human conception of time is characterized by the finitude of our being toward death. It is this finitude that is at odds with the eternal conception of time, which is hidden in the concept of time as an endless series of moments. It is at such a moment that time seems to be entirely present at once; at such a moment, one establishes the future and the past as if they are fully available. However, the finitude of time is at odds with such an endless perspective; human time has a direction from birth to death, and is therefore finite.

It is with these insights that we can distinguish three interrelated problems of legal time that all boil down to Heidegger's criticism of the ordinary conception of time: (1) human time cannot be stopped; (2) whereas one can travel through clock time, one cannot traverse human time; and (3) eternity and mortal human time shall never meet.

[61] M. Heidegger, *The Concept of Time* (New York: John Wiley and Sons, 1991), p. 20E.

[62] M. Heidegger, *Sein und Zeit* (Tubingen: Max Niemeyer Verlag, 2006).

[63] Heidegger, *The Concept of Time*, p. 21E. [64] B. Adam, *Time* (Cambridge: Polity Press, 2004), p. 58.

[65] L. Alweiss, "Heidegger and 'the Concept of Time,'" *History of the Human Sciences* 15, no. 3 (2002), p. 122.

[66] Hoy notes that even in Heidegger there seems to be a contradiction at work as to the question of which form of time comes first, Dasein or temporality: "the neo-Kantian effort in *Being and time* to 'deduce' one from the other turns out to be unnecessary." Hoy, *The Time of Our Lives*, p. 23.

Stoppage Time

The case of *Paposhvili* v. *Belgium* before the ECtHR dealt with the expulsion of a migrant suffering from leukemia to Georgia.[67] The migrant had resided in Belgium since 1998, had unsuccessfully applied for asylum, and subsequently on several occasions attempted to regularize his stay and that of his family. It did not help his case that he had been convicted of several (severe) criminal offenses and served more than a few prison sentences. In 2006 – while in prison – he was diagnosed with a life-threatening form of leukemia. When his health started to deteriorate, he received medical treatment, which was intensified from 2010 onward.

In 2007, his first request for regularization on medical grounds was filed, which was refused because he did not fall within the scope of the Belgian rules due to his criminal record. In 2008, he tried this again, the procedure lasting several years. The main argument in these procedures was that his expulsion to his country of origin would lead to a situation contrary to Article 3 ECHR: the right not to be subjected to torture or inhuman or degrading treatment. He did not fear that he would be subjected to treatment contrary to Article 3 by the Georgian government itself, rather, he feared that he would not receive the proper medical treatment for his disease and that this would result in a situation of inhuman or degrading treatment.

In 2012, Mr. Paposhvili was requested to report to the Belgium Aliens Office's medical service for a medical checkup. The report stated that his leukemia had stabilized after several cycles of chemotherapy and that he was being monitored closely. Referring to the relevant case-law of the ECtHR, the report concluded that his expulsion to Georgia would not meet the severity threshold of Article 3 ECHR because there was no direct threat to his life. At that time, the relevant criterion for meeting the minimum level of severity under Article 3 in medical expulsion cases was that there should be a direct threat to the migrant's life as a result of a critical condition or the very advanced stage of the illness. In other words, the migrant should prove that he was "close to death" and that expulsion would lead to being subjected to treatment contrary to Article 3. Eventually, the case of Mr. Paposhvili went all the way to the ECtHR, whose Grand Chamber in 2016 adjusted the relevant criterion for medical cases. The Court decided that situations in which a migrant was exposed to serious, rapid, and irreversible decline in their state of health, resulting in intense suffering or to a significant reduction in life expectancy (paragraph 183), could also lead to a breach of inhuman and degrading treatment in Article 3.

This case was hailed by scholars as a significant ruling that changed the narrow approach to Article 3 removal cases.[68] Indeed, the Court lowered the threshold in such medical cases of expulsion from "close to death" to "serious, rapid and irreversible decline." Yet, it is not the changed threshold that makes this case so telling for the role and meaning of legal time. It is clear that in this line of case-law, no matter the exact criterion, the Court makes use of human time. After all, both criteria refer to the foresight of the medical situation of the particular individual; they entail an assessment of the future of this migrant and the foreseeability of their further decline and/or unfortunate death. Basically, if you read the story of Mr. Paposhvili and the years of proceedings in which he attempted to regularize his

[67] ECHR December 13, 2016, *Paposhvili* v. *Belgium*, 41738/10.

[68] See e.g. L. Peroni, "*Paposhvili* v. *Belgium*: Memorable Grand Chamber Judgment Reshapes Article 3 Case Law on Expulsion of Seriously Ill Persons," *Strassbourg Observers*, 2016.

stay in Belgium on the basis of his medical situation, this story can be read as one of waiting until his medical situation deteriorated enough to forbid his expulsion. Clearly, the Court ultimately decided in this case that *if* Mr. Paposhvili would have been expelled to Georgia in 2016, this would have violated Article 3 ECHR. In this sense, the case can be read as an excellent example of how the lapse of human time can be referred to in legal time. After all, both the "close to death" and the "serious, rapid and irreversible decline" criteria refer to irreversible and finite character of human time.

Notably, the case simultaneously shows how human time is structurally and fundamentally different from the reference to it in legal time. *If* Mr. Paposhvili had been expelled; the conditional clause is the crux of the matter here. What makes the *Paposhvili* ruling so revealing for our purposes is not the technical discussion about the exact criteria in medical cases but the realization that hidden behind the use of this conditional conjunction in the ruling of the Court is the most extreme example of the abyss between legal time and human time: at the time of the ruling of the ECtHR, Mr. Paposhvili had already died. As a matter of fact, Mr. Paposhvili had died as early as June 7, 2016, a little more than half a year before the Court ruling. On June 20, 2016, however, his family expressed the wish to pursue the proceedings, therefore presenting the Court with a problem. Normally, the Court only permits the next-of-kin to pursue an application if they have a legitimate interest. There are many cases in which that could be conceivable but presumably not in Mr. Paposhvili's. After all, he asked the Court not to be deported since such an expulsion would deteriorate *his* medical situation, not the situation of his family. Also, the family of Mr. Paposhvili had already been regularized quite some time ago. Consequently, it appeared as if the family members had no legitimate interest in pursuing the application. In fact, Article 37, paragraph 1 of the Convention stipulates that an application may be struck from the list if the applicant does not intend to pursue the application; the matter has been resolved or for any other reason the continuation of the examination is no longer justified. The provision, however, also allows for continuation of the examination where the Court finds that the respect for human rights so requires.

It was quite remarkable that the Court decided not to strike the case from the list and simply deemed it unnecessary to determine whether the family had a legitimate interest. Taking ample time to emphasize its point, the Court explained that the case affected a serious question of the interpretation of the Convention, seen already from the referral of the case to the Grand Chamber. Thus, the impact of the case went beyond the particular situation of Mr. Paposhvili. As such, the contrast between the two conceptions of time could not possibly have been starker. It is precisely the individual, mortal, and thus finite time of the migrant that is the core of the matter in this case, and this entails rather a detailed scrutiny of the medical situation of Mr. Paposhvili. In fact, the old "close to death"“criterion basically consisted of an assessment of the amount of time this individual migrant had left before he would die. In the new criterion, the proximity to death has been replaced by the irrevocable decline of the claimant's time. Yet, both stem from the mortality of the individual, after all, someone's decline is irrevocable because it will (eventually) lead to his death. The irony is that the procedure focussed on the irrevocable decline or the physical death of the individual – yet, the *actual* death of this particular individual during the procedure did not hinder the Court in proceeding with his case.

However, the point here is not to criticize the Court for pursuing the case of Mr. Paposhvili after he had deceased. After all, the judgment certainly changed the case-law and had an important impact on cases of migrants in similar situations. The case, rather, serves to show how two mutually exclusive conceptions of time can be at work simultaneously in a legal procedure. Whilst developing a criterion explicitly based on the finitude of human time, the Court was confronted during the proceedings exactly with the irrevocable finitude of such time. Precisely in an endeavor to establish a general criterion based on the mortality of human beings, it was confronted with the death of the individual who was at the heart of the legal question in the first place. Yet, from the perspective of general legal time, there was obviously no problem. The Court indeed established its criterion, which has been of use ever since that moment. With Heidegger's analysis in mind, however, it could be said that the Court sought for a criterion of "just before death" or "irrevocable decline" that was eternal: a criterion that stops the movement of time, in which the future and past of the individual are entirely present. As useful as such criterion may be, legally speaking – again I am not arguing against this usage of time – it is important to realize that it does not capture the process to which it refers. After all, the difference between an ordinary conception of time and human time is that human beings are defined by their mortality, that human time is finite. Yet, the paradox is that even though our experienced human time is defined by mortality, one cannot experience once dead.[69] The experience of one's mortality is impossible to describe, while it is possible to pinpoint someone else's death on a calendar, or to relate that event to a moment in time. That, however, objectifies precisely what cannot be objectified, the irrevocability of human time, the finitude of one's own time.

The crux of the matter is that human time cannot be stopped, whilst the time of the clock can be paused. This is what so paradoxically comes to light in the case of Mr. Paposhvili: the procedure about the application of the "close to death/irrevocable decline" criterion to his case took too long because his death occurred during the time of the procedure. Despite the fact that legal procedure and the moment of a decision suggest that they stop time and assess the matter from an eternal position, in reality, time goes on. This can certainly lead to problems, for it does not only apply to explicit questions of mortality, or death, it emerges in many instances. In the next chapter, I argue that this problem of time is at the heart of the difference between a just and unjust usage of time in migration law.

Time Traveling

The second problem that can be discerned based on Heidegger's criticism of ordinary time can be described using the rather mysterious figure of the "declaratory act," not to be confused with the "constitutive act." The classic example of the declaratory act in migration law is refugee protection. Recital 21 of the Qualification Directive states: "The recognition of refugee status is a declaratory act." This means that recognition of a refugee status does not make the migrant into a refugee, it declares them to have been such from the first moment of leaving their place of origin.[70] "He does not become a refugee because of recognition, but

[69] At least that is what we assume, since no one who has experienced it lives to tell the story. "Why should I fear death? If I am, then death is not. If Death is, then I am not. Why should I fear that which can only exist when I do not?," as Epicurus famously puts it. See for a critical discussion of this point in Heidegger, Alweiss, "Heidegger and 'the Concept of Time,'" p. 126.

[70] Boeles et al., *European Migration Law*, p. 298. This is one of the basic principles of refugee law, see also G. S. Goodwin-Gill and J. McAdam, *The Refugee in International Law* (Oxford: Oxford University Press, 2007), p. 51.

is recognized because he is a refugee."[71] This seemingly simple statement has large consequences for the asylum procedure and for the notion of time in it. It implies that the moment a migrant fullfils the condition of the Refugee Convention, they are a refugee. The question of the legal recognition of the refugee is illustrative for the second problem of legal time: the problem of time traveling.[72] What does it mean that a refugee is recognized as being the subject that they already are?

To answer this question, we have to ponder a little longer on how the declaratory act and its antonym – the constitutive act[73] – relate to one another. A naïve understanding of the difference between declaratory and constitutive acts proposes that some people would belong to a certain category or identity already before, or even entirely without the involvement of, the law, whereas others are merely created by the law and have no existence outside it. Constitutive would then be a legal creation, whereas declaratory would merely recognize what already existed. This would suggest that there are entities that find their way into law, which have meaning within law, without the law qualifying them. If that was true,[74] it certainly is not true for categories of people. After all, the criteria for who *is* a refugee are provided by the law and are not external to it. Moreover, not everyone who claims to be a refugee will be recognized as such. Not only does the law stipulate who qualifies as a refugee and who does not, it is determined in the legal procedure whether a person indeed fits into the legal criteria. Hence, we have to distinguish between the criteria and the application of these criteria. The difference between a declaratory act and a constitutive act does not relate to a difference in criteria: both use legal criteria not *extralegal* criteria.

The difference therefore must be sought in the application and the temporal effect it has. If the legal act merely has a prospective effect, it is a constitutive act, if it has a retrospective and a prospective effect, the act is declaratory. Yet, only when the procedure to establish whether the person falls within a certain legal category takes a long time does the difference become particularly striking. Only when there is a long time between the moment of the application and the moment of the decision does the temporal effect of a declaratory act becomes apparent. Compare, for example, refugee recognition with the situation of recognition of EU citizenship. Just as with recognition of a refugee, recognition of an EU citizen is a declaratory act. The difference is, however, that whereas recognition as a refugee is often time-consuming and complicated, recognition of an EU citizen is fairly simple. Article 2 of the Citizenship Directive (2004/38) stipulates that an EU citizen is any person that is a

[71] United Nations High Commissioner for Refugees, *Handbook and Guidelines on Procedures and Criteria for Determining Refugee Status* (Geneva: United Nations High Commissioner for Refugees, 2011), paragraph 28.

[72] The problem of time traveling, described here on the basis of Heidegger's analysis of time, could just as well have been done on the basis of Bergson's theory of time. Basically, his criticism of a mechanistic conception of time is that time is reversible because if the basic parts remain the same, there is nothing to prevent their return to the initial position.

[73] The question of a declaratory act and constitutive act also plays in international public law in the question whether new entities become states when they fulfill the criteria for statehood or when they are recognized as such by other states. See e.g. S. Talmon, "The Constitutive versus the Declaratory Theory of Recognition: Tertium non Datur?," *The British Year Book of International Law* 75, no. 1 (2005).

[74] We have already seen that it is not true for time, which is always qualified time. It certainly is not true for territory either, see L. Bosniak, *The Citizen and the Alien* (Princeton, NJ: Princeton University Press, 2006), and also Bosniak, "Being Here"; Leti Volpp, "Imaginings of Space in Immigration Law," *Law, Culture and the Humanities* 9, no. 3 (2013). Would it be true for weight or distance?

national of a Member State. Hence, if a migrant shows a valid identity card or passport of one of the Member States, the procedure is completed. So, the procedure of establishing whether someone is an EU citizen is in general nigh "automatic"; it takes almost no procedural time. In such a case, the retrospective effect of a declaratory act is not very revealing, since the retrospective character does not affect any substantial lapse of time between the application and the recognition.

This is different in the case of refugee recognition because such a procedure can sometimes take years. Consequently, the moment that the refugee is recognized as being such, then they were a refugee throughout the entire procedure. Only in such a situation are we confronted with an inconsistency of time: because of the application of legal criteria, someone becomes a refugee, yet this has an effect even before these criteria were applied. When a procedure takes a long period of time, the declaratory status of a refugee leads to a situation of time traveling. Time is traversed in at least two ways: into the future and into the past. The former becomes apparent when analyzing the difference between the refugee and the predecessor, the asylum seeker. If a refugee must be understood to be someone who has been a refugee from the moment that they applied for recognition as a refugee, the question arises as to the status of someone who has already asked for recognition, yet not recognized as a refugee at that particular moment. Such an asylum seeker may after all turn out to have been a refugee in the first place, yet, it could transpire that they are not a refugee. This implies that an asylum seeker is someone who is at the same time potentially a refugee and potentially not a refugee, a situation reminiscent of Schrödinger's hypothetical cat experiment.[75]

Here we again encounter the legal attempt to construct an expectation of the future, albeit, this expectation of the future has double potentiality, we must reckon with two scenarios at the same time. What is typical about the asylum seeker is that these two expectation or potentialities are present at the same time in the same legal persona. Certainly, if the law constructs the expectation of the future of a migrant for their long-term residence status, two possibilities are also apparent (will they stay or will they go?). Nonetheless, the point is that under the Long-Term Residence Directive, the law constantly tries to divide these two expectations into different legal categories. A separate category for migrants with a temporary objective, another category for nontemporary residence, long-term residents fall into yet another category, while family members are treated different again, and so on. Such a legal double potentiality is not restricted to asylum law; the parallels with, for example, an accused in criminal law are apparent. Nevertheless, the point is that in a procedure, both potentialities structure the way in which the subject is treated. In other words, this implies a form of time traveling, reckoning with multiple possible future scenarios that have implications in the present.

[75] The problem of refugee recognition is reminiscent of Schrödinger's hypothetical cat experiment. If a cat is put in a box, in which it could by means of a device be killed or not in a given period of time, and the chances that it would die equals the chances that he would remain alive, then this would imply that without looking into the box, the cat is both alive *and* death, at least if you follow an observer-driven interpretation. The difference, however, is that the question of whether the cat is dead or alive is ontologically speaking to be distinguished from the observer, whereas such is not the case with refugee recognition. After all, the category of "refugee" is a legal category, and therewith dependent on legal recognition. Thanks to Galina Cornelisse and Frances Gilligan for pointing this out to me.

These two potentialities have clear legal consequences. From the rights granted to the potential refugee, the right to stay in the territory is certainly the most important. Recital 25 of the Procedure Directive states that "In the interest of a correct recognition of those persons in need of protection as refugee . . . every applicant should have an effective access to procedures . . . [which] should normally provide an applicant at least: the right to stay pending a decision by the determining authority." Article 9 of this same directive stipulates that the asylum seeker may remain in the territory for the sole purpose of the procedure until the moment that the determining authorities have made a decision. This right to remain does not constitute an entitlement to a residence permit (Article 9, paragraph 1). It makes perfectly clear that the potentiality of being a refugee is enough to grant the asylum seeker the right to remain in the territory.

Conversely, the consequences of the potential for the nonrefugee are also clearly indicated in the Directive. Article 31, paragraph 8 of the Procedure Directive stipulates under which circumstances Member States may provide for an accelerated examination procedure or border procedure. In most of these situations, serious doubts exist that the migrant is a refugee (Article 31, paragraph 8, subparagraphs a–g). If that is the case, the entire procedure to establish whether someone is a refugee may be done within a short period of time (which must be reasonable, Article 31, paragraph 9), and entry into the country can be refused. The ground for this must be that the presumption is that there is proof that the applicant is not a refugee. When eventually the procedure comes to an end, time can also be traversed retrospectively: refugee status can be granted from the moment of the asylum application. This form of antedating is yet another temporal mechanism to deal with the problem of lapse of time. It consists of time traveling and it is important to see that it presumes an actual moment in someone's life, as every form of time traveling does. It is this reference to such a moment that enables the traversing of time in two directions: from the past toward the present and from the present toward the past.[76] Probably the best-known example of this in popular culture is the *Back to the Future* movies, in which the protagonist Marty McFly travels through time to his past and future. This science fiction is only conceivable because we relate his present (1985) to the past (1955) and his future (2015). We constantly know that we are situated in the past or future because the "real present" is situated in 1985, even if we watch the movie in 2020. Thus, it is impossible on the sole basis of a certain calendar date to determine whether it is past, present, or future. This has to do with the simple fact that such a temporal understanding presupposes a human perspective, a human who discerns what is the present. Moreover, an eternal conception of time is presumed that stops time (in 1985), therefore leaves no room for succession, and at once oversees the different moments in time (1955 and 2015). This eternal conception of time is the presumed temporality of the film, whenever you watch it, the "present" of the film remains stuck in 1985, despite its subject of time traveling.

Still, what does this time traveling demonstrate about the functioning of legal time? First of all, the question of the declaratory character of refugee status could just as well be used to illustrate the previous point about the difference between eternal and finite time. The declaratory status is based on the moving image of eternity, to use Plato's description. It is this eternal element that provides a strong moral fundament to the protection of the potential refugee during the procedure. It is the eternal character that suggests that the

[76] Ricoeur, *Time and Narrative*. Volume 3, p. 106.

question of refugee protection exceeds the power of the state to define who can qualify as a refugee. Moreover, it emphasizes the moment from which the refugee is in need of protection, which is the moment they leave their home territory. The longer the procedure has taken, however, the more far-fetched it becomes to pretend the asylum seeker in fact has been a refugee all the time, to act as if no time has lapsed since the moment of the application for asylum. The antedating functions as a proper legal solution to deal with the temporal inconsistency that can lapse for quite some time before one is legally determined to be the refugee that they have always been.

There is a certain overlap between the discussion of the issue of time traveling and the previous discussion of mortality, as described in the case of Paphoshvili, yet the two are not exactly the same. The point here is that it might be possible to traverse time in the legal procedure but remains impossible to traverse human time, given the arrow of human time. However useful and fair it may appear to be to use a retrospective temporal mechanism that antedates a residence permit, human time has already lapsed and cannot come back. If an asylum seeker has spent four years waiting for the outcome of an asylum claim, those years will not return. Similarly, an ever-lasting procedure for family reunification with a child will not restore childhood. Restrictive measures during the asylum procedure that were based on anticipation of a future that turned out to be correct cannot be undone. Of course, our understanding and perception of the past may change, just as that one may apologise, seek restitution or reconciliation, or demand damages; nevertheless, what remains impossible is to *undo* the events of the past, or to know what will happen in the future.

Confined to Eternity

The third problem that follows from the difference between finite and eternal time can probably be best described using the cases of *K.* v. *the Netherlands* and *H. F.* v. *Belgium* before the European Court of Justice of the EU (CJEU).[77] This case dealt with two asylum claims that were both rejected on the basis of Article 1F of the Refugee Convention, excluding people from refugee protection if they had committed a crime against peace, a war crime, or a crime against humanity. For the sake of argument here, it is enough to focus on one of their stories. The case of H. F. concerns an Afghan national who arrived in the Netherlands on February 7, 2000, and requested asylum, an application that was rejected on May 26, 2003, because he had apparently directly or indirectly participated in war crimes or crimes against humanity. In 2006, the Dutch authorities refused to grant him a temporary residence permit, after which time the decision of 2003 became final and H. F. was subjected to an entry ban. The story of H. F. continued to Belgium, where he and his daughter settled in 2011 and he endeavored in subsequent years to regularize his stay. In the meantime, his daughter became a Dutch national, after which event he repeatedly and unsuccessfully requested family reunification with his daughter on the basis of her EU citizenship. Moreover, he was frequently ordered to leave the Belgian territory. After the last rejection, however, the authorities no longer attached an order to leave Belgium to the decision.

The nucleus of the legal issue at stake in this case was one of time. The Belgium government followed the Dutch authorities in arguing that it had become apparent that H. F. had committed crimes falling within the scope of Article 1F of the Refugee

[77] CJEU May 2, 2018, *K.* v. *the Netherlands* and *H. F.* v. *Belgium*, C-331/16 and C-366/16.

Convention. "In particular, he had participated in war crimes or crimes against humanity, or had given orders, given his position, to commit such crimes. The representative therefore considered that the threat to one of the fundamental interests of society represented by the presence of an individual such as H. F. … is inherently permanent and current" (paragraph 33). In other words, because the migrant had committed or was likely to have committed very serious crimes in the past, his presence on the territory still constituted a threat to public order – it still constituted, that is crux of the matter, a form of temporal differentiation by means of temporality, as discussed in Chapter 1. According to the governments of Belgium and the Netherlands, "an assessment of that individual's future conduct is not, in such circumstances, important, given the nature and gravity of the crimes concerned, and consequently there should be no need to demonstrate whether the threat stemming from the conduct of that individual, and the risk of repetition of such conduct ('re-offending'), is plausible and present" (paragraph 33). With this stance, the representatives of the governments basically distanced their position from the regular framework of public-order crimes. Indeed, a threat of public order is a well-accepted ground for not granting a residence status or withdrawing one already given. In such cases, the question is, according to well-established case-law of the CJEU, as we have seen in Chapter 1, whether an "actual threat" exists and not merely a threat in the past. With this criterion, EU law basically requires assessing whether there is a *current* threat at the moment of the decision, even if a long period of time has lapsed since the crime has been committed. Consequently, the central question in this case became whether this regular public order criterion was also applicable to 1F situations. Or to put this question bluntly in more mundane terms: can someone be excluded forever – or eternally, to link it immediately to Heidegger's discussion – from residence entitlements because a crime has been so serious that the threat to society is deemed to remain present forever?

To be sure, this question is rather pressing. These migrants are often situated in a legal limbo: they are not allowed to enter, nor can they be sent back to their country of origin because of the principle of *nonrefoulement*.[78] Regularly, they see no other option than to stay on the territory, just as in the case of H. F., who had lived unlawfully for eleven years in the Netherlands and then stayed another seven years in Belgium. Can such a situation last forever or can the threat to society allegedly embodied by these people diminish over time, legally speaking, so that the migrant can be allowed to enter after a lapse of time?

Basically, the Court takes a middle position in this judgment. A government may not automatically conclude from the mere presence of an Article 1F–excluded person in its territory that this constitutes a genuine, present, and sufficiently serious threat to one of the fundamental interests of society. There should be an individual assessment, taking into account the gravity of the crimes committed; the time that has lapsed since the crime; and importantly, "the persistence in him of a disposition hostile to the fundamental values enshrined in Articles 2 and 3 TEU, capable of disturbing the peace of mind and physical security of the population" (paragraph 66). Hence, it is conceivable that someone is excluded permanently, yet this cannot be concluded automatically, and from this follows that it should be assessed from time to time whether the threat is still present.

[78] J. Reijven and J. van Wijk, "Caught in Limbo: How Alleged Perpetrators of International Crimes Who Applied for Asylum in the Netherlands Are Affected by a Fundamental System Error in International Law," *International Journal of Refugee Law* 26, no. 2 (2014).

Although the Court maintains that there should be an actual assessment of the threat even in cases of very serious crimes, it restricts its scope to the public-order framework that follows from EU law. It does not deal with the question of whether an eternal – or indefinite – exclusion from society would be fair in the first place. In order to exactly pinpoint the distinction between eternal time and the finitude of human time, it is worthwhile pondering a little longer precisely on that discrepancy. It appears that there is something in the difference between the two that is to be distinguished from the previously raised issues: human mortality and the arrow of time.

It is a point that would very well apply to the situation of Article 1F–excluded persons but has been raised in the context of lifelong imprisonment in a judgment by the other European Court, the ECtHR.[79] In that case, the Court was confronted with the question of whether a lifelong imprisonment could violate Article 3 ECHR: the right not to be tortured or treated inhumanly or degradingly. The Court held that such a lifelong sentence in itself does not constitute a violation of that provision, as long as there is the possibility of reviewing whether the punishment is still proportionate after a long period of time (twenty-five years). This does not serve to say that an imprisonment that lasts longer will be disproportionate, the Courts stress that if imprisonment is effectively lifelong, this does not necessarily have to mean that there would be an issue under Article 3. There should, in other words, be a prospect of release, not an actual release. After all, the Court stresses

> [i]t is axiomatic that a prisoner cannot be detained unless there are legitimate penological grounds for that detention. As was recognised by the Court of Appeal in Bieber and the Chamber in its judgment in the present case, these grounds will include punishment, deterrence, public protection and rehabilitation. Many of these grounds will be present at the time when a life sentence is imposed. However, the balance between justifications for detention is not necessarily static and may shift in the course of the sentence. What may be the primary justification for detention at the start of the sentence may not be so after a lengthy period into the service of the sentence. It is only by carrying out a review of the justification for continued detention at an appropriate point in the sentence that these factors or shifts can be properly evaluated.
>
> (paragraph 111)

So, the balancing exercise for the justification of detention is not static, it changes over time. However, what exactly is the role of time here? In a rather succinct consideration, the Court brilliantly captures the difference between eternity and human time:

> Moreover, if such a prisoner is incarcerated without any prospect of release and without the possibility of having his life sentence reviewed, there is the risk that he can never atone for his offence: whatever the prisoner does in prison, however exceptional his progress towards rehabilitation, his punishment remains fixed and unreviewable. If anything, the punishment becomes greater with time: the longer the prisoner lives, the longer his sentence. Thus, even when a whole life sentence is condign punishment at the time of its imposition, with the passage of time it becomes – to paraphrase Lord Justice Laws in Wellington – a poor guarantee of just and proportionate punishment.
>
> (paragraph 112)

There we have it, eternal exclusion does not only not take into the equation changes that occur over time, more significantly, it simply cannot be put into terms of human time. After

[79] ECHR July 9, 2013, *Vinter and Others* v. *the United Kingdom*, 66069/09, 130/10, and 3896/10.

all, someone can die tomorrow or in half a century, and this makes quite a difference for the weight of the punishment. Eternal time and human time, never the twain shall meet.

These two cases of the two European courts provide us with two important conclusions. The first is the categorical difference between eternal time and human time, the former is difficult to express in terms of the latter. Eternal time does not move, whilst human time is clearly characterized by succession. The second conclusion follows from this observation and relates to the way that this tension is operationalized in law. The two judgments exemplify that as regards the exclusion of residence entitlements or the deprivation of liberty, simply equating eternal time with human time is unjust. Legal time should at least leave open the possibility to assess how the exclusion relates to the lapse of time. The solution that the ECtHR puts to the fore is to introduce a recurrent deadline – the legitimacy of the prison sentence should be reviewed from time to time.

Conclusion: Grasping Human Time

In this chapter I have focussed on the slithering character of legal time. I have identified three interrelated characteristics of human time that come if one scrutinizes the difference between eternal and mortal time, that is at work in legal time. The first is that human time cannot be stopped. This does not only imply that time is finite, as we have witnessed in the case of Mr. Paposhvili, it also means that human time inevitably moves forward from birth to one's inescapable death.

This problem is closely related to the problem of time traveling, the second conundrum of time, albeit that in the latter, the emphasis is slightly different. There can be good reasons, as we have seen with the figure of refugee recognition, to make use of a form of legal time traveling, for example, by antedating a residence permit. Nonetheless, it is important to realize that such time traveling in actual human time is impossible. The figure of time traveling presumes an actual moment in time on which the future and past can be determined; one cannot *actually* go back to the past and forward to the future (which would then no longer be the past or future). Nor is it possible to undo wrongs in the past. Human time has a direction; not only is it impossible to pause human time, one cannot go back in time (nor forward). Time lost in a long legal procedure, for example, cannot be regained or relived, no matter what the antedating of the permit might suggest.

The third problem is the irreducible relationship between eternal and mortal time. As exemplified by the discussion of asylum seekers exempted from refugee protection on the basis of Article 1F Refugee Convention and the considerations on lifelong imprisonment, eternal time does not fit the frame of human time. If one wants to eternally exclude someone, it is unclear how long this will actually last. Infinite exclusion in terms of human time can be short or long, depending on how long one actually lives. After all, the concept of eternity does not allow for considerations about length of time – in eternity, time does not move, everything is present simultaneously.

We have concluded with Bergson that the success of legal time is to be found in its exterior character. Legal time is based on a fixed moment in which time does not lapse, whilst at once different moments can be discerned that can be connected to one another creating a linear relation. From this moment, the past, present, and future can be discerned, which can be traversed in different directions. Legal time has exteriority, therefore, it is external to the process to which it nevertheless seems to refer, it lacks, however, succession.

The success of legal time, in other words, is its usage of eternal time. Bergson, however, reminds us that the reference to a process is always inadequate, it is qualitatively different from what it refers to. We have seen this in the discussion of formal and material criteria used to refer to the process of migrants living within a certain territory. Two dominant approaches – jus domicilii and jus nexi – both ultimately fail to grasp such a process. After all, in purely formal clock time criterion, the reference to the individual lived experience over time is lost, whilst in a pure material criterion, the reference to lapse of time eventually vanishes. A material time criterion has, in other words, exteriority but lacks succession, it can be met at any moment. To be sure, this does not lead to the conclusion that jus domicilii and jus nexi have no argumentative force but merely that they have a difficult relationship with lapse of time.

The vices of legal time that I have identified in this chapter – the inability to fully grasp processes in legal terms and the strain between eternity and mortality – are in the first place imperfections of legal time. They simply reflect the Janus face of legal time, which can never be fully resolved. In the next chapter, I will argue that these problems will become vices in the moral sense, if the value of finite, irreversible, and unstoppable human time is neglected. I argue that if one takes the succession of human time seriously, this in itself constitutes an argument for inclusion of long-term residing migrants.

3

Jus Temporis or the Immigrant's Right to Human Time

> The life span of man running toward death would inevitably carry everything human to ruin and destruction if it were not for the faculty of interrupting it and beginning something new, a faculty which is inherent in action like an ever-present reminder that men, though they must die, are not born in order to die but in order to begin.
>
> Hannah Arendt, *The Human Condition*, 1958 AD

> "You don't show enough respect for what is written, and you're changing the story," the priest said. "The story contains two important statements by the door-keeper about admission to the Law – one at the beginning and one at the end. In one place it says that he cannot grant the man admission now, and in the other it says that this entrance was intended only for the man. If there were any contradiction between these two statements you would be right and the door-keeper would have deceived the man. But there isn't any contradiction. On the contrary, the first statement actually implies the second. One might almost say that the door-keeper exceeded his duty in holding out to the man the prospect of perhaps being admitted sometime in the future. The door-keeper's duty seems to have consisted at that time solely in turning the man away . . ."
>
> Franz Kafka, *The Trial*, 1925 AD

When does the skillful manipulation of time in law insidiously turn into unjust manipulation? With that pressing question I concluded Chapter 1 of this book, a chapter in which I highlighted the sophisticated ways in which human and clock time are used in migration law to control and differentiate the presence of migrants within a certain territory. In Chapter 2, I described two temporal challenges that follow from the tension between legal and human time, with which any conception of legal time inevitably has to deal. These are related to the problem of the extension of time – I opened this topic in Chapter 2. In this third chapter, I endeavor to answer the persistent question: Are there temporal limits to the manipulability of time in law? Or, to make it more tangible: Can governments simply change terms for naturalization from five years to, for example, twenty years? Can asylum procedures be extended indefinitely? Can a migrant be sent back to their "home country" after having resided in their "host country" for more than fifty years? Can unlawfully residing migrants be permanently excluded from lawful residence, even when they cannot be returned to their country of origin?

In this chapter, I argue that the "temporal governance" that was analyzed in Chapter 1 finds its normative and legal limitation in "the right to human time," or in what one could call a jus temporis.[1] This right to human time boils down to, as I argue in this chapter, the

[1] Elizabeth Cohen has coined the term jus temporis in relation to questions of citizenship, focussing on American debates about eligibility for citizenship, see Cohen, "Citizenship and the Law of Time in the

legal acknowledgment of the particular characteristics of human time that I spelt out in Chapter 2. The right to human time recognizes the difference between clock and human time, taking into account that the latter is finite, cannot be turned back, nor stopped.

I first discuss the temporal governance of long-term residing migrants, and argue that the peculiar character of human time in such governance should be acknowledged. At the heart of the analysis in this book is the legal control of the presence of migrants within a given territory by means of legal time. It is important to keep in mind that the object of legal control is therefore not so much the mere presence of migrants but their presence over time, the process of migrants living within a certain territory. However obvious this might seem, it is precisely this process that complicates legal matters, as we have seen in the problems described in Chapter 2. I argue that we should take these problems and the peculiar character of human time seriously.

In European law, there is clearly a tendency to take human time seriously – at least to a certain extent – for certain categories of migrants, with stark historical differences. After having observed that in (European) law, durable presence on the territory generally leads to ethical and legal claims for inclusion, I discuss the existing rationales for such claims for inclusion of long-term migrants (ius domicilii and ius nexi). Given the contemporary meritocratic tendency to focus on migrants who behave well, and exclude those who do not live up to material integration criteria, I suggest that mere time spent on a territory itself constitutes an argument for inclusion. By pointing at the formal/material problem, I discuss how arguments for inclusion based on integration and ties miss the temporal reference to human time spent on a territory. Endeavoring to supplement the existing arguments, I therefore plead that inclusion based on rootedness should not be confused with inclusion based on integration. As I argue, such a rationale boils down to the acknowledgment that human time cannot be turned back, which makes time spent within a territory irreplaceable. I demonstrate that the acknowledgment of this temporal argument, the rootedness, is already at work in (European) migration law, most notably by means of deadlines for long-term residence permits and naturalization.

Subsequently, I discuss the implications of jus temporis regarding waiting time in procedures; regarding the temporary character of lawful presence; and regarding the question: How long may an unlawfully residing migrant continue to be excluded from entitlements while they remain present within the territory? I argue that the specific characteristics of human time leads to three normative limitations to the exclusion of entitlements for migrants within a given territory. These limitations can already be found in (European) migration law: countdown deadlines for procedures; end terms for withdrawal of residence status; and regularization of long-term unlawfully residing migrants.

Taking Human Time Seriously: Rootedness

In Chapter 1, I praised clock time for its ability to reference processes that inevitably take place in time. In Chapter 2, however, I described a paradox that appears when one attempts to grasp the process of a migrant's presence on a given territory in legal criteria. If put in clock time, it no longer refers to the experience of the individual's life, yet when it is

United States." My emphasis in the meaning and application of principle is slightly different from that of Cohen, as discussed later in this chapter.

expressed in material criteria, it risks losing any reference with the presence on the territory over time. In this sense, both criteria suffer from the problem of extension, they both presume exteriority from the life of the migrant, at the risk of becoming so external to the process that they describe that they no longer refer to it. One might object that this is purely a theoretical problem, after all, in practice, both criteria will be used together. The material criteria will enable reference to the life of the migrant, while the clock time will make sure that the migrant has spent time on the territory. However, I will argue here that in practice this can lead to problems – that is to say, when taking the jus domicilii and jus nexi argument too strictly, precisely the life of the migrant risks becoming forgotten. This becomes most apparent in the case of long-term residing "criminal migrants." The aim of this chapter is to explicate within the existing body of literature and rules and regulations a normative, temporal argument that serves or can serve as a balance to the force of temporal governance.

Domicile and Ties

As mentioned in Chapter 1, temporal differentiation is an important means for immigration and citizenship control. Just as it can be used to provide migrants with stronger rights over time, it can be employed to exclude migrants from claims for stronger entitlement, for example, regarding the long-term resident status or naturalization, because the respective residence is deemed to be "temporary." Alternatively, residence can be held to be discontinuous, thereby excluding it from the scope of such forms of stronger residence entitlements.

Yet, the possibilities to exclude migrants from (stronger) residence entitlements by means of legal techniques of temporal differentiation might seem endless, there are strong normative arguments against such long-term exclusion. There is a large body of literature that argues that the presence within a certain territory provides migrants a normative right to inclusion into the citizenry, or at least a status as permanent resident or "denizen."[2] Importantly, the focus in this literature is on spatial normativity, or as Linda Bosniak dubs it, "ethical territoriality."[3] The most prominent and explicit protagonist of such a view is political theorist Michael Walzer, who defends the political inclusion of those who are present within the territory of a democratic community. "The processes of self-determination through which a democratic state shapes its internal life, must be open, and equally open, to all those men and women who live *within its territory*, work in the local economy, and are subject to local law."[4] As Bosniak claims, this appreciation of territorial

[2] S. Benhabib, *The Rights of Others: Aliens, Residents and Citizens* (Cambridge: Cambridge University Press, 2004); Bosniak, "Being Here"; Carens, *Immigrants and the Right to Stay*; M. Dummet, *On Immigration and Refugees* (London: Routledge, 2001); Hammar, "Legal Time of Residence and the Status of Immigrants"; D. Kostakopoulou, *The Future Governance of Citizenship*, Law in Context (Cambridge: Cambridge University Press, 2008); Rubio-Marín, *Immigration as a Democratic Challenge*; Shachar, "Earned Citizenship"; Shachar, *The Birthright Lottery*; S. Song, "The Rights of Noncitizens in the Territory," in *Immigration and Democracy* (New York: Oxford University Press, 2018), pp. 173–88; Song, "The Significance of Territorial Presence and the Rights of Immigrants"; N. Walker, "Denizenship and Deterritorialisation in the European Union" in *A Right to Inclusion and Exclusion? Normative Fault Lines of the EU's Area of Freedom, Security and Justice* ed. H. Lindahl (London: Hart Publishers, 2009), pp. 261–72; Walzer, *Spheres of Justice*.

[3] Bosniak, "Being Here." [4] Walzer, *Spheres of Justice*, p. 60, emphasis added.

presence is embraced by many political theorists on the rights and recognition of noncitizens within a given society.[5] Territorial presence makes a difference, normatively speaking.[6] Yet, can we distinguish within existing arguments (hidden) temporal normativity, and, what can temporality add to such spatial arguments?

The long-term exclusion from full citizenship of a migrant who is present on a territory has been criticized for creating second-class citizens or denizens and undermining normative ideals of democratic participation and equality.[7] As Dora Kostakopoulou succinctly puts it "a polity that prides itself on its democratic underpinnings, therefore, cannot exclude segments of its population from influencing or taking part in decision-making that affects them thereby treating them as a subject class."[8] While such migrants de facto participate in society by virtue of their work, their role in a web of social interactions, or by means of paying tax, they remain excluded from full citizenship. Moreover, they cannot take part in the drafting of laws or designate the future of the community, although they are subjected to those laws and de facto part of the community.[9] "Political justice is a bar to permanent alienage," Michael Walzer famously argued.[10]

For such reasons, countries provide legal possibilities for full inclusion of long-term residing migrants (either by naturalization or a full package of rights for long-term residing migrants).[11] Important arguments for inclusion are formulated as jus domicilii or jus nexi, which I will both further scrutinize to elucidate the role of time in these arguments.[12] In the

[5] Bosniak, "Being Here," p. 393. See also Song, "The Significance of Territorial Presence and the Rights of Immigrants"; Song, "The Rights of Noncitizens in the Territory."

[6] In the conclusion I will return to this issue of territorial presence when discussing the shifting border, see Shachar, *The Shifting Border*.

[7] There is a large body of literature focussing on democratic arguments for and against inclusion of those present within a territory, see for an overview R. Bauböck, "Democratic Inclusion," in *Democratic Inclusion: A Pluralist Theory of Citizenship* (Manchester: Manchester University Press, 2018). I will not discuss all of these democratic arguments here; my focus is purely on temporal arguments about the presence of migrants within a certain territory. For this reason, I also leave aside Bauböck's argument of "stakeholder citizenship," which is clearly a temporal argument but not focussing on territorial presence. Bauböck focusses on all of those whose interests will be affected by a collectively binding decision, including "individuals whose circumstances of life link their future well-being to the flourishing of a particular polity," R. Bauböck, "Stakeholder Citizenship and Transnational Political Participation: A Normative Evaluation of External Voting," *Fordham Law Review* 75, no. 5 (2007).

[8] Kostakopoulou, *The Future Governance of Citizenship*, p. 104.

[9] "Democratic decision making and the flourishing of a political community require the involvement of all the community – not simply a segment of it," ibid., p. 126.

[10] Walzer, *Spheres of Justice*, p. 61.

[11] See for the latter e.g. Song, "The Significance of Territorial Presence and the Rights of Immigrants"; E. F. Cohen, *Semi-citizenship in Democratic Politics* (Cambridge: Cambridge University Press, 2009). The most prominent European example of stronger rights for long-term residing migrants is the earlier discussed Long-Term Residence Directive, see for an overview of possibilities to acquire nationality in European countries, R. Bauböck et al., *Acquisition and Loss of Nationality: Policies and Trends in 15 European States*. Volume 1: Comparative Analyses (Amsterdam: Amsterdam University Press, 2006); R. Bauböck et al., *Acquisition and Loss of Nationality: Policies and Trends in 15 European States*. Volume 2: Country Analyses (Amsterdam: Amsterdam University Press, 2006).

[12] Miller observes that there is broad agreement among authors who write about immigration that being present in a society for a considerable period creates a very strong if not indefeasible case for permanent inclusion, but there is some disagreement about exactly why long-term presence should entail permanent inclusion. Miller discerns "subjected to coercion," "adverse possession," and "social membership," Miller, *Strangers in Our Midst*, p. 123. In this chapter, I focus mostly on the argument of "social membership"

most radical version of the domicile principle, rights and entitlements would simply be linked to presence on the territory, thereby eliminating "formal citizenship as a mechanism of domination based on birth privilege and labour segmentation within a territorial community."[13] Emphasis is on the actual presence, on human mobility and people's right to choose their civic and political home and, indirectly, the rules of the association that govern them.[14] As we have seen in the previous chapter in Shachar's plea for inclusion based on jus nexi, the actual presence on the territory is also at the heart of the argument. She argues that inclusion of long-term residing migrants acknowledges and gives legal meaning to what in fact has already taken place.[15]

Both principles give normative value to the de facto situation of either the residence of the migrant or the ties that have developed over time. The actual "social membership" of the migrant that has developed over time is crucial in such arguments, as we already discussed in Chapter 2. As Carens puts it "in these contexts the term 'social membership' evokes the sense that being a member of a society involves a dense network of relationships and associations."[16] In the jus domicilii approach that Carens defends, time within the territory is a proxy for the social connections that migrants will inevitably develop over time, as we have seen. Such connections are assumed and as we will see in the next paragraph, precisely this assumption is the weak spot of such an argument.

Yet, it is important to first explicate that both jus domicilii and jus nexi refer to the process from an exterior position, as we have seen with Bergson. With this perspective, the process is stopped; and at once different moments can be discerned, which can be linked to one another. For example, based on the moment of arrival on the territory and the moment a residence permit was granted, it can be established how much time has elapsed between them. In other words, both principles presume time as a moving image of eternity, in which nothing passes and everything is present at once. At the moment of the legal decision, the past and the future are made present, so that they can be overseen and evaluated. Consequently, the exteriority in the moment of the legal decision is the obvious prerequisite for any judgment of the ever-moving life of the legal subject.

for it most clearly exposes the temporal argument that I want to expose. See for a critical analysis of the relationship between territorial presence and social membership in prevailing argument for inclusion, Ochoa Espejo, "Taking Place Seriously." Ochoa Espejo instead proposes "ius situs," a normative argument that links duties and certain rights to the mere fact of "being there."

13 Bauder, "Jus Domicile," p. 188. Kostakopoulou would link inclusion on the basis of domicile with the intention to reside permanently or at least indefinitely, Kostakopoulou, *The Future Governance of Citizenship*, p. 114. This intention is, however, a rather problematic proxy for the future, as Motomura has shown, someone intending to stay temporarily might after a lapse of time rather stay indefinitely, and the other way around, H. Motomura, "We Asked for Workers but Families Came: Time, Law and the Family in Immigration and Citizenship," *Virginia Journal of Social Policy & the Law* 14, no. 1 (2006).

14 Kostakopoulou, *The Future Governance of Citizenship*, p. 119.

15 Shachar, "Earned Citizenship," pp. 131–2.

16 Carens, *The Ethics of Immigration*, p. 164. Rubio-Marín equally writes:

> The basic idea is that membership is first, and above all, a social fact, determined by social factors such as living, working or raising a family and participating in the social and cultural life of a community. The moral relevance of this social fact and what it implies (dependency on society for the protection of rights and the development of a meaningful life project, as well as subjection to the decisions collectively taken in it) is the fundamental basis for the claim to full inclusion.

Rubio-Marín, *Immigration as a Democratic Challenge*, p. 21.

Moreover, the reference to lapse of time in jus domicilii and jus nexi arguments is quite innovative. The advantage of jus domicilii and jus nexi over single-moment deadlines such as jus sanguinis and jus soli is, after all, that the former enables reference to the life of the person within the territory (as it develops after birth), whilst the latter freezes a certain moment in time that is incapable of accommodating change. Jus domicilii and jus nexi therefore have an argumentative force in themselves, and as we have seen, their use is clearly visible in European migration law.

Still, I hold that both jus domicilii and jus nexi risk silently privileging an immovable image of eternity in their reference to the life of the migrant within the territory. These arguments tend to neglect the finite, unstoppable, and irreversible character of human time, which has a normative value in itself. I will elucidate this claim by discussing one particular case of migrants in which both jus domicilii and jus nexi fall short in their protection of the (prolonged) inclusion migrants, even though these cases clearly refer to migrants who have had a long-term stay within the territory: the case of long-term residing "criminal migrants." It is in discussing such cases that the normative value of human time becomes the most apparent.

Can a Criminal Alien Integrate?

In March 2017, Len van Heest, at the age of fifty-nine, was deported from Canada to the Netherlands. Van Heest migrated to Canada when he was seven months old and had not left the country since.[17] His parents had applied for Canadian citizenship but forgot to request this status for their son. At the age of sixteen, van Heest was diagnosed with bipolar disorder. His lawyers contended that the long list of offenses that he had committed was directly related to his mental illness – over forty criminal convictions for uttering threats, assault, and mischief. He had never attempted to become a Canadian citizen but had he wanted to naturalize, these convictions would have nonetheless obstructed his application. In any case, van Heest lived for fifty-seven years in Canada, while officially still being a Dutch national. When he was deported to his "home country," he was effectively sent to a country where he had never set foot, where he did not speak the language, or had any effective social network. Would a jus nexi or jus domicilii argument have prevented such an expulsion of this type of long-term residing migrant?

To answer that question, it is helpful to have a look at the case-law of the European Court of Human Rights (ECtHR) in which the jus nexi approach can be clearly identified. This case of van Heest does not stand on itself. There is a long list of cases regarding the expulsion of long-term residing migrants for public-order reasons in European law, especially in the case-law of the ECtHR on the right to private life under Article 8.[18] As discussed in Chapter 2, in this case-law, time spent on the territory plays an important

[17] The case received quite a lot of media attention in both Canada and the Netherlands, see e.g. www.cbc.ca/news/canada/british-columbia/len-van-heest-update-deportation-netherlands-1.5021185.

[18] This pattern coincides with policies in North American and European countries that aim to denationalize as a tool of counterterrorism, see e.g. A. Macklin and R. Bauböck, "The Return of Banishment: Do the New Denationalisation Policies Weaken Citizenship?," *EUI Working Paper*, RSCAS 2015/14 (2015). See for a critical historical overview, M. B. Dembour, *When Humans Become Migrants: Study of the European Court of Human Rights with an Inter-American Counterpoint* (Oxford: Oxford University Press, 2015), pp. 161–95, and the referred cases therein.

role in balancing the interests of the state and the migrant. In key cases such as *Boultif*, *Üner*, and *Maslov*, the Court provides a framework for the proportionality assessment in which the breach of public order should be weighed against the family and private life of the migrant. The latter is expressed, most importantly, in the solidity of social, cultural, and family ties with the host country and with the country of destination. In *Üner*, the Court stressed the importance of time in such an assessment:

> The Court has held the "Boultif criteria" to apply all the more so (*à plus forte raison*) to cases concerning applicants who were born in the host country or who moved there at an early age (see *Mokrani* v. *France*, no. 52206/99, § 31, 15 July 2003). Indeed, the rationale behind making the duration of a person's stay in the host country one of the elements to be taken into account, lies in the assumption that the longer a person has been residing in a particular country, the stronger the ties with that country will be whereas the ties with the country of nationality will become weaker. Seen against that background, it is self-evident that the Court will have regard to the special situation of Aliens who have spent most, if not all their childhood in the host country, were brought up there and received their education there.[19]

From this follows that if a migrant arrived at a young age and lived continuously in the host country without having any ties with their "country of origin," only substantial reasons of public order may outweigh this in the proportionality assessment under Article 8.[20] The reasoning of the Court clearly resonates arguments of social membership in scholarly literature.

Nonetheless, this does not imply that mere time spent within the territory means that a migrant can no longer be expelled: it is *qualified* time that is weighed in the balancing exercise under Article 8 of the European Convention on Human Rights (ECHR); and the quality of the time is pivotal. Despite the starting point that the duration of a person's stay in the country leads to the assumption that they have over time developed strong ties in the host country, and weakened ties in the country of origin, it is certainly possible under Article 8 ECHR to expel a long-term residing migrant if they have simply not behaved properly. Or as Marie Dembour concludes in her study, "[w]hen Humans become Migrants ... the idea that states can expel Aliens has much stronger hold on the Strasbourg case law than the wish to see migrants being treated like nationals whenever possible."[21] The case-law therefore equally exemplifies that a jus nexi argument will often

[19] ECHR October 18, 2006, *Üner* v. *the Netherlands*, 46410/99, paragraph 58.

[20] E.g. ECHR January 12, 2010, *A. W. Khan*, 47486/06; which is not to say that it is impossible, since the expulsion of the brother of A. W. Khan, A. H. Khan was held not to be in violation of Article 8, see ECHR December 20, 2011, *A. H. Khan*, 6222/10.

[21] Dembour, *When Humans Become Migrants*, p. 185. And it seems to have become easier, see e.g. the dissenting opinion of Turkovic in ECHR September 14, 2017, *Ndidi* v. *the United Kingdom*, 41215/14. Or as Başak Çalı and Stewart Cunningham conclude, "In particular, the more serious the criminal offence committed by the long-term migrant, and the older the long-term migrant, the less likely is the Court to attach significant weight to their length of residence," B. Çalı and S. Cunningham, "The European Court of Human Rights and Removal of Long-term Migrants" in B. Çalı, L. Bianku, and I. Motoc, *Migration and the European Convention on Human Rights* (Oxford: Oxford University Press, 2021), pp. 159–74. A similar development can be witnessed in cases regarding withdrawal on the basis of public order of EU citizens, see most notably: CJEU April 17, 2018, *Vomero*, C-424/16, C-316/16. See for a discussion of this development, B. Ryan, "Selective Citizenship: How the Court of Justice Linked Security of Residence to Integration," *European Journal of Migration and Law* 21, no. 3 (2019), pp. 374–99.

not protect the migrant from expulsion.[22] If a migrant is a regular offender or has committed a very serious crime, and does not change life for the better, it is rather unlikely that expulsion will amount to a violation of Article 8 ECHR.

Notwithstanding the cases in which an appeal to Article 8 was successful, it seems that the lack of protection of Article 8 in cases of long-term residing migrants who commit criminal offenses has to do with the specific rationale behind the case-law of private life under Article 8. The point is, to put it bluntly, that the criminal offense is conceived to be an indication of the lack of integration of the migrant, whilst it is precisely the integration of the migrant that should be balanced with the criminal offense. In the *A. H. Khan* case, the Court makes this explicit:

> Furthermore, the applicant's private life in the United Kingdom, as observed by the Tribunal, has been constrained by his convictions and spells in prison. Whilst he was mainly educated in the United Kingdom and has worked, he does not appear to have established a lengthy or consistent employment history. In short, and despite the length of his stay, the applicant did not achieve a significant level of integration into British society.[23]

This starting point also follows from the line of case-law in which a considerable amount of time has lapsed since the last offense; if in such cases the migrant has changed their life (considerably) for the better, this has a lot of weight.[24] Such "reintegration" into society is particularly important if the offense is committed by a minor.[25] So, here we have it, a jus nexi argument is as such not a very strong argument against expulsion of long-term resident migrants who commit (serious) crimes: the breach of public order precisely signifies the deficiency of character, the absence of which could have saved the migrant in the first place. To come back to the case of Len van Heest, it is rather unlikely that he would have been protected under the current case-law of Article 8 ECHR.

This jus nexi approach is not restricted to the case-law of the ECtHR, it can also be found in the recent case-law of the European Court of Justice of the European Union (CJEU) on the expulsion of long-term residing European Union (EU) citizens in light of the Citizenship Directive (Directive 2004/38), albeit hidden under the surface. Scrutiny of EU case-law on this matter reveals even more clearly the meritocratic character of jus nexi; and the stark difference with a formal time criterion. The preamble of the Citizenship Directive stipulates that the "greater the degree of integration of Union citizens and their family members in the host Member State, the greater the degree of protection against expulsion should be"; a starting point that is rather similar to the case-law under Article 8 ECHR, as we have seen. This system of protection consists of a gradual system that can be found in Article 28, in which clock time functions as the proxy for integration. At first sight, it seems, therefore, to be the opposite of the jus nexi approach in the case-law of the ECtHR, and represents the formal time criterion, as discussed in the previous chapter. In such a formal

[22] That is to say, on the basis of the case-law of the Court, one cannot estimate in how many cases migrants made a successful or unsuccessful appeal to Article 8 to prevent their expulsion; nevertheless, jus nexi clearly does not provide for an absolute rule in this case-law.

[23] ECHR December 20, 2011, *A. H. Khan*, 6222/10, paragraph 41.

[24] See most notably, ECHR September 20, 2011, *A. A.* v. *the United Kingdom*, 8000/08; and ECHR September 14, 2017, *Ndidi* v. *the United Kingdom*, 41215/14.

[25] ECHR September 20, 2011, *A. A.* v. *the United Kingdom*, 8000/08, paragraph 68.

approach, the reference to the individual integration of the migrant is replaced by a general time criterion, thereby losing connection with the actual integration of the migrant.

The first paragraph of Article 28 consists of the general provision that stipulates criteria for a proportionality assessment that is reminiscent of the Boultif criteria. The second paragraph specifies that only serious grounds of public policy or public security may justify an expulsion of EU citizens with permanent residence as meant under Article 16. The third paragraph stipulates that the protection of EU citizens who have resided for more than ten years in the Member State is considerably strengthened. In those cases, only *imperative* grounds of public security may justify the expulsion.[26]

It is in these last two steps of the scale that a formal time criterion is used, while leaving out any explicit reference to material criteria of integration. After all, the permanent residence of the second paragraph can only be obtained after five years of residence; and as soon as this status is obtained, it simply seems to function as a proxy for the strong integration of the EU citizen. That is to say, Member States may require third-country nationals to comply with integration measures before granting the long-term resident status in addition to terms of residence. Yet, the integration is not explicitly linked to the time of residence within the territory. This becomes even more clear in the presumption in the third paragraph of the provision in which the ten years of residence is also clearly a formal time criterion (without any reference to integration or integration criteria). Long-term continued residence generally serves as a proxy for stronger integration and resultingly, stronger protection against expulsion.

However, how could such a presumption relate to a criminal conviction? Does that serve as a token of deficient or broken integration, just as in the case-law of the ECHR? Can the presumption of integration in the formal time criterion be falsified by the "actual lack of integration" that allegedly follows from the criminal conviction? These questions were explicitly dealt with by the CJEU in the case of *Vomero*.[27] The question first arose as to whether time spent in prison could count toward continuous residence under the gradual protection against expulsion of Article 28, a clear example of temporal differentiation by means of qualification, as has been discussed in Chapter 1. In other words, the question was whether the period spent in prison would count toward the ten-year period that would qualify for the strong protection of paragraph 3. That question, the Court held, could not be answered in general terms; it must be assessed after looking at all the particularities of the case whenever the question of expulsion arises. With this, the Court basically added a jus nexi assessment to the formal time criterion of ten years. Instead of assuming that the ten years of time functioned as proxy for integration, it has now transpired that in the case of time spent in prison, it is no longer simply time spent on the territory that counts for integration.[28] The question as to the relationship between a prison sentence and integration became even more pertinent when discussing the question of whether the conviction might impede the protection under paragraph 3:

> Indeed, particularly in the case of a Union citizen who was already in a position to satisfy the condition of 10 years' continuous residence in the host Member State in the past,

[26] Boeles et al. have questioned whether the Court in fact distinguishes between "serious grounds" and "imperative grounds" in its case-law; Boeles et al., *European Migration Law*, p. 59.

[27] CJEU April 17, 2018, *Vomero*, C-424/16, C-316/16.

[28] In the Tsakouridis case, "integration" was still used to protect the individual, as Ryan observes, in later case-law, protection under the ten-year rule is conditional on social integration, see Ryan, "Selective Citizenship."

> even before he committed a criminal act that resulted in his detention, the fact that the person concerned was placed in custody by the authorities of that State cannot be regarded as *automatically* breaking the integrative links that that person had previously forged with that State and the continuity of his residence in that State for the purpose of Article 28(3)(a) of Directive 2004/38 and, therefore, depriving him of the enhanced protection against expulsion provided for in that provision. Moreover, such an interpretation would deprive that provision of much of its practical effect, since an expulsion measure will most often be adopted precisely because of the conduct of the person concerned that led to his conviction and detention.

There we have it indeed, if the conviction would automatically break the integrative links with the host country, then this provision would lose its practical effect. Still, what the Court subsequently does in this judgment is precisely this, it diminishes the practical effect of the provision by replacing the ten-year term by a jus nexi assessment. The referring court should assess whether those "integrative links with that State are solid – including from a social, cultural and family perspective, to the point where, for example, the person concerned is genuinely rooted in the society of that State." In case the integrative links of the EU citizen with the host country appear not to have been solid, this breaks the continuity of the ten-year period *retrospectively*, consequently denying the strong protection afforded under paragraph 3.

The case of *Vomero* shows, in other words, the exclusionary aspects of a meritocratic approach like jus nexi.[29] It is clear that jus nexi can be a forceful tool to obtain stronger protection or full citizenship for migrants, since it might retrospectively acknowledge social ties and rootedness that have grown over time spent within the territory. Yet, the case of criminal migrants demonstrates that similar arguments can also be used for exclusionary purposes, simply because the qualification of the time spent on the territory excludes those who do not meet the criteria.[30] Does this mean then that there is no strong claim for (prolonged) inclusion of long-term residing "criminal migrants" after lapse of time?

Looking at jus domicilii, would an argument based on this principle work for long-term residing migrants who have committed crimes? Of course, it is conceivable to construct a jus domicilii argument that consists of an end term (just as this is possible for jus nexi) after which the withdrawal of residence status is no longer possible; or precluding the withdrawal of the status based on public order, as Kostakopoulou argues with her concept of "anational citizenship."[31] Yet, arguments for jus domicilii, or "ethical territoriality" as Linda Bosniak has coined it, are often part of postnational or transnational frameworks that focus on human mobility. As Kostakopoulou puts it "[c]itizenship based on domicile puts emphasis

[29] Ayelet Shachar acknowledges this, she has called the focus on merits a paradigm shift "selecting by merit, not origin," which is rather dystopian: "While we cannot read the tea leaves of the changed landscape of citizenship, we can sketch the contours of the dystopian future to which it could potentially lead: a neo-mercantilist world in which the rush to fast-track prized recruits undercuts other important commitments." A. Shachar, "Selecting by Merit: The Brave New World of Stratified Mobility," in *Migration in Political Theory* (Oxford: Oxford University Press, 2016), p. 176. See for the more broader philosophical critique on meritocracy M. J. Sandel, *The Tyranny of Merit: What Becomes of the Common Good* (London: Allen Lane, 2020).

[30] As the extensive body of literature on the problematic character of integration conditions in migration and citizenship practices demonstrates, see Chapter 2, footnote 56.

[31] Kostakopoulou, *The Future Governance of Citizenship*, p. 137.

on the bonds of association that individuals establish as members of a society. As such, it is consonant with human mobility and peoples' right to choose their civic and political home and, indirectly, the rules of the association which govern them."[32] The decision of a person to leave their state of origin, to settle elsewhere, and to become a full member of that community should be fully respected by the home and host states. It seems from this perspective that jus domicilii fits well with a framework that enables human mobility.[33]

Bosniak, however, has critiqued jus domicilii precisely because it is useful as an argument for those who are in the host country, while the mere fact of being in the host country continues to be a limited commodity.[34] I would agree with Bosniak that – despite its transnational suggestion that privileges human mobility instead of territorial borders – jus domicilii in practice reinforces the territorial conception of citizenship and therewith the sovereign power to determine who may enter the territory, and – just as importantly – who should leave the territory. The argumentative strength of the jus domicilii is to be found in its arguments for the treatment of migrants that reside within the territory. That said, it is not as forceful as arguing in favor of entry of migrants to the territory or against their removal from the territory.[35]

To clarify why jus domicilii is not such a powerful argument against removal from the territory of long-term residing migrants, it is important to emphasize that this conception precisely attempts to break necessary links between someone and the territory or the community, contrary to jus sanguinis, jus soli, or even jus nexi. Basically, jus domicilii is based on the assumption that residence rights have no essentialist or necessary link with a certain territory. The link between residence and territory is contingent in this argument, it could just as well be a link with yet another territory. Although, the de facto residence within a given territory should be legally acknowledged, it does not present a strong case against expulsion, just as it is not a strong argument for entry. Jus domicilii is purely an argument based on *presence*, based on the situation as it is at a given moment in time, not on links with the territory that have established over time. Jus domicilii, one could say, lacks temporality, it does not take into account the past and future, it is purely based on a conception of the present.

The case of long-term residing migrants who breach public order accordingly indicates the limits of both jus domicilii and jus nexi approaches to residence entitlements. The former because the link between territory and residence is criticized, the latter for its meritocratic focus on ties. Certainly, this does not mean to say that one could not conceive of jus domicilii or jus nexi in ways that would lead to inclusion of long-term residing "criminal migrants." After all, it is possible to operationalize both in ways that would make it impossible to withdraw a residence status in such cases. Still, I contend that there is an important temporal argument to be made in favor of the (prolonged) inclusion of "criminal migrants," an argument merely based on the value of human time.

32 Ibid., p. 119.

33 In the words of Bauder, "Jus domicilii thus accommodates the mobility of people between communities and territories," Bauder, "Domicile Citizenship, Migration and the City," p. 82.

34 Bosniak, "Being Here."

35 The former problem has led Harald Bauder to argue in favor of (semi)open borders to accompany his claim for jus domicilii, Bauder, "Jus Domicile."

Jus Temporis as Ground for Inclusion of Rooted Migrants

In the following, I argue that regarding the legal inclusion of long-term residing migrants next to jus domicilii and jus nexi, a third argument should be discerned that is closely related but different from the others. This argument is based on the human time of a migrant within a given territory and I will dub this, to emphasize the relationship and difference with the former two, jus temporis. I argue not only that such argument should be discerned, normatively speaking, from jus domicilii and jus nexi but moreover that it is already at work in (European) migration law. In other words, that to fully understand the functioning of existing rules regulating the presence and withdrawal of (long-term) residing migrants, a third type of argument existing alongside those based on mere presence and those on existing ties is inexorable.

This argument of jus temporis is based on the assumption that human time spent on a territory is significant. Elizabeth Cohen first coined the term jus temporis in her analysis of the role of time in the norms for eligibility for citizenship in the USA.[36] Cohen shows that temporal rules have been present in the laws regulating US citizenship since the early days and were important to the establishment of sovereignty. Nowadays, rules of time still play an important role in the acquisition of nationality. Cohen praises the specific quality of clock time to refer to a multitude of different and often contradictory norms at the same time. "Time is both an administratively convenient and normatively freighted way to represent our most deeply held-and sometimes fiercely contested-beliefs about citizenship."[37] Moreover, as has been mentioned before, clock time refers to processes that happen in time, without pinpointing the exact relationship with these processes. The virtues of time highlighted in Chapter 1 indeed make time a rather functional criterion for the regulation of citizenship for newcomers.

Yet, I would argue that such an understanding of jus temporis is susceptible to the difficulties described in Chapter 2: most notably relating to the specific characteristics of human time. I maintain that it is important to emphasize the meaning and normative value of human time in any argument for jus temporis. Moreover, I argue that its normative value not only relates to the acquisition of citizenship but equally to waiting time in procedures; to the temporary character of long-term residents; and to the regularization of unlawfully residing migrants.

Human time within a certain territory matters, legally and normatively – that is the fundament of jus temporis. It shares this starting point with jus nexi and it is also widely acknowledged in contemporary (European) migration law, as seen in Chapter 2. Migrants put down roots over time – commonly referred to as becoming "rooted." As mentioned in Chapter 2, the EU Long-Term Residence Directive emphasizes in preamble 6 that the main criterion for acquiring the status of long-term resident should be the duration of residence in order to show that the person has put down roots in the country. In other words, the prerequisite for stronger residence entitlements is residence on the territory over time, in which time the migrant becomes rooted. A similar starting point can be discerned in the case-law of Article 8 ECHR. In Chapter 2, however, we witnessed that legally speaking this "rootedness" is rather elusive, it is difficult to grasp in legal terms. In a formal time criterion, based on straightforward clock time, the reference to the process of rootedness as it

[36] Cohen, "Citizenship and the Law of Time in the United States."
[37] Cohen, *The Political Value of Time*, p. 79.

develops in time is clear, yet the specific circumstances of the case are lost. Whilst in a pure material criterion, eventually the reference to successive time risks being lost. After all, one could meet such material criterion at any point, or never. Reminiscent of Bergson's critique I have argued in Chapter 2 that both a formal and material criterion of time lose something in their reference to rootedness. In the following, I argue that the case of long-term residing migrants that breach public order shows what such attempts lose: reference to the finite, irreversible, and unstoppable character of human time.

To better appreciate the role of human time, it is necessary to ponder a little longer on the concept of rootedness that is at the basis of claims for stronger residence entitlements. The anthropologist Liisa Malkki has criticized this concept because it conceptualizes the relationship between people and place as sedentary.[38] Taking her cue from the French philosopher Gilles Deleuze and psychoanalyst Felix Guatarri, Malkki argues that the conceptualization of nations and national identities is often peculiarly arborescent.[39] Such arborescent metaphors suggest that human beings belong in one place, where they grow their roots, develop, blossom, and eventually die. This "sedentary bias" is used to position migrant's rootedness in their "place of origin," even when generations have been born in their new country. Rootedness in such an arborescent conception somehow naturalizes the relationship between the migrant and their "country of origin," therewith neglecting any changes that might develop over time.[40]

An argument for inclusion based on rootedness indeed risks falling into the same trap. After all, if roots are not linked to a territory in an essentialist manner, if one can grow new roots over time elsewhere, how can roots then be an argument against forced mobility? When one accepts the possibility of becoming rooted over time, then this means that one does not assume a necessary link between people and place. This implies, however, that one could have multiple roots, and thus become "rerooted" elsewhere. Contemporary international mobility might indeed serve as proof that people can resettle in another country.[41] Certainly, one can argue that people should not be forced to leave the places where they have (developed) roots, but then the argumentative force shifts from roots to people's right to choose their home. Would this mean then that only an essentialist conception of

[38] L. Malkki, "National Geographic: The Rooting of Peoples and the Territorialization of National Identity among Scholars and Refugees," *Cultural Anthropology* 7, no. 1 (1992); see for another critique of the prioritization of stasis in migration theory, T. Nail, *The Figure of the Migrant* (Stanford, CA: Stanford University Press, 2015), and more generally in philosophy the work of Rosi Braidotti on the nomadic subject R. Braidotti, *Nomadic Subjects* (New York: Columbia University Press, 2011).

[39] The problem might not be the natural bifurcation metaphors per se, after all roots could also be understood as rhizomes, lacking a central origin and binary bifurcation, as Deleuze and Guattari have argued in "Rhizomes" in the introduction to their seminal work G. Deleuze and F. Guattari, *A Thousand Plateaus: Capitalism and Schizophrenia*, trans. B. Massumi (London: The Athlone Press, 1996).

[40] See also H. Ghorashi, "Negotiating Belonging beyond Rootedness: Unsettling the Sedentary Bias in the Dutch Culturalist Discourse," *Ethnic and Racial Studies* 40, no. 14 (2017).

[41] A similar argument is put to the fore by David Miller,

> The point, then, is that anyone who migrates has to make a trade-off between the costs that are born (by their family as well as by themselves) in moving to a new country and the potential benefits stemming from the opportunities available there. That many people either do or would wish to migrate shows that the costs of moving – including the breaking off of many established social ties – are not so high as to form a decisive obstacle.

Miller, *Strangers in Our Midst*, p. 124.

rootedness could come to rescue the long-term residing migrant here? So, the roots that develop over time make the migrant *really* belong to the place, in a somehow essentialist manner? That would be rather paradoxical indeed, since such rootedness could just as well be used to exclude the migrant by arguing that they still belong to their country of origin, as Malkki demonstrated.

Jus domicilii, on the other hand, precisely seems to start from this criticism of Malkki. It can be understood in a similar vein to critique birthrights such as jus soli and jus sanguinis, which link someone in a similar essentialist manner to a certain territory at the moment of birth, making use of what Elizabeth Cohen has called a single-moment deadline, thus neglecting any actual developments after that moment. As we have seen earlier, jus domicilii bases itself, instead, on actual presence, rather than on roots or any other particular essentialist relationship between people and territory. For this reason, it is not a strong argument against expulsion from the territory (or in favor of entry into the territory, as Bosniak shows). In the end, both the possibility of becoming rooted over time as well as the legal acknowledgment of mere presence critique the essentialist relationship between territory and person and seem to lack strong argument against the expulsion of the person from the same territory.

That is to say, I would argue against such an interpretation of rootedness. In the previous discussion, I have deliberately left out the element of human time in order to show its argumentative force. In the following, I focus on the argument of human time by making an analytical distinction between rootedness and integration. I argue that in (European) migration law, a conception of rootedness is at work that is not susceptible to Malkki's essentialism critique, nor can it be equated with integration that suffers from the meritocratic problem of jus nexi.

As seen earlier, birthright citizenship has been criticized for prioritizing the moment of birth and not taking into account what happens subsequently in a human life. Jus domicilii and ius nexi are attempts to deal with this problem of time by focussing on time actually spent within a given territory. Malkki's critique of rootedness fits into this tradition of thought, for it problematizes the essentialist link between territory and roots, thereby stalling lapse of time and neglecting what has happened after birth. Yet, it leaves open the possibility of another conception of rootedness, a conception that is based on the lapse of *human* time within a territory.

In Shachar's pledge for jus nexi, the retrospective acknowledgment of the actual social fact of membership that has inevitably developed over time is a clear reference to durable human time and temporality. It takes into account and gives legal meaning to what has already occurred in a specific human life. She refers to this process as an incremental process in which one's center of life gravity shifts over time.[42] However convincing this argument is in many cases, we have seen that it is not helpful for long-term residing migrants who have committed crimes. The case of "criminal migrants" raises the question of what the meaning of this "incremental process" is. After all, the concept of an incremental process suggests indeed that this is an inevitable consequence of the lapse of time, therewith reflecting a teleological conception of the arrow of time, as discussed in the Introduction as a chrono-logic of rights. It might not happen at the same pace for everyone, but if one waits long enough, one would see a process in which slowly everyone's center of

[42] Shachar, *The Birthright Lottery*, p. 169.

life gravity shifts. However, the case of "criminal migrants" seems to contradict this starting point. At least, if one takes a normative stance on what social membership signifies. In such a scenario, the criminal behavior of the migrant is, as European law testifies, a token for *lack of integration.*[43]

In other words, if one understands this incremental process at the basis of the jus nexi principle as *integration*, and if one considers breach of public order as a lack of integration, then it is clear that criminal migrants falsify the incremental process. The case of criminal migrants shows that mere lapse of time and integration have no necessary link. As discussed in Chapter 2, this typifies the problematic relationship between time and a material integration criterion. Such material criterion could be met at any moment, or never. In the end, a material integration criterion has no necessary relationship with lapse of time, as we have seen.

Still, I would argue that long-term residing criminal migrants have a strong argument for (prolonged) inclusion or against expulsion. Even though an incremental process might not be the most accurate description, I do think that a strong case can be made that argues that the longer one resides, the stronger a claim for residence becomes. I would say that time spent on the territory has an arrow, a direction. Yet, this arrow does not point to more integration, better ties, or more participation as a full blown and active citizen. It is not the progressive temporality of a chrono-logic of rights, as Bonnie Honig has put it,[44] which Anne McNevin on her turn criticized for its colonial logic.[45] The crux of the matter is to clarify that the reference to time in this argument is not the reference to clock time but to human time. It is precisely the generality of clock time that is misleading here, it is, after all, simply not the case that people become rooted at the same pace, or develop ties in a comparable manner. Nor does this process necessarily lead to a stronger – or even essentialist or unbreakable – bond with a certain territory. The point is merely that someone's time spent on the territory is irreversible and finite and that, in itself, is an argument to be taken seriously. The arrow of time I am referring to is the direction of human time, from birth to death.

The case of Len van Heest exemplifies *in extremis* the normative value of human time. Obviously, one could just as well argue that van Heest has developed ties to Canada whilst he lacks effective ties with his "home country" and that such a nexi-argument should prevent him from being expelled to the Netherlands. Nonetheless, the force of that argument should not be overstated, as we have seen, because of the mere fact that people across the world constantly move to countries with which they have no ties. If people can become rooted, they can start over again elsewhere. The point is, however, that they cannot *really* start from scratch, in the sense that their time cannot be turned back. Len van Heest

[43] One could argue that a system is conceivable in which only the ties count and bad behavior or criminal activities cannot break these ties. Of course, it is possible, yet I think the meritocratic way of reasoning easily leads to a system that includes migrants that behave well, therewith silently presuming that migrants that do not behave well do not deserve inclusion, or even deserve to be excluded. I have argued in this paragraph that European migration law testifies to this pattern in its treatment of "criminal migrants," see also Shachar, "Selecting by Merit."

[44] The "chrono-logic of rights" focusses "on the right as it is seen by those who privilege as its meaning its capacity to be extended and tapped in certain ways that fulfil what they see as its true function or promise, regardless of its operations." Honig, *Emergency Politics*, pp. 54–5, see further the paragraph in the Introduction on the arrow of time.

[45] McNevin, "Time and the Figure of the Citizen."

cannot start again in the Netherlands as if he has not spent fifty-seven years of his life in Canada, as if he is still seven months old. These fifty-seven years of clock time are not just a proxy for a process, they also constitute the lived time of an individual, time that is irreversible and finite. Clock time might be objective and general while referring to individual lives; it cannot be equated with a person's experienced human time. Disguising as the measurement of time, the case of van Heest shows that the clock changes what it supposedly measures. It is precisely in this difference that the skillful manipulation of legal time finds its limits.

If one complements jus domicilii with the perspective of finite and irreversible human time, a strong argument against expulsion of long-term migrants emerges. The mere focus on presence in a jus domicilii argument is timeless, it does not take into account the lapse of human time, and seems to presume that someone can always start anew elsewhere – as if no time had lapsed. Such a perspective is Platonic, as we have seen in Chapter 2; it uses an eternal conception of time that is at odds with the finite conception of human time. Yet, if one complements the argument with finite human time, it becomes evident that lapse of human time on a territory makes a difference. Not because time on the territory creates an essentialist, permanent tie or bond with the territory or community but simply because the time spent on the territory is undeniably bound to the life and the time of the specific human being. No matter how the life of the migrant is assessed from the perspective of integration, no matter how the migrant might have behaved in their time on the territory, it is simply a fact that they have spent time on the territory. Accordingly, the greater proportion of finite time spent by the migrant within a territory, the stronger a claim for inclusion will be.

The same applies to the argument of jus nexi that takes the de facto situation as a starting point for its analysis. Retrospectively acknowledging the actual membership of those who have resided on the territory over a period of time is not enough, the case of criminal migrants exemplifies this point. One should also retrospectively acknowledge that even if the migrant has not behaved well in that time, they have spent precious time on the territory and this should not be ignored. The argument of jus nexi gains strength when it is understood as referring to human time, instead of clock time.

Hence, rootedness signifies the entanglement of presence within a territory with the lapse of finite and irreversible human time of someone's life. This constitutes, next to arguments of integration or mere presence, an argument for (prolonged) residence entitlements. Indeed, the question remains what value will be granted to this jus temporis based on rootedness in a specific case. This will vary, countries will have different appreciation of the value of human time. Moreover, this value undergoes historical changes, I argue in the conclusion of this book that it is currently under pressure in European migration law. However, I simply wish to bring to the fore the value of human time for migrants that become rooted, and recognize that it easily becomes forgotten when focussing too much on clock time. That risk applies to jus nexi and jus domicilii, but equally to a conception of jus temporis that simply equates the use of time with lapse of clock time.

Concrete Implications of Jus Temporis

As mentioned in the Introduction, Carol Greenhouse argues that it is law's cultural role to preserve the indeterminacies of time that are the result of the tension between individual lifetimes and the time of the social order.[46] What I have so far described as problems, or failures, can just as well be seen as the sites on which the law creates solutions to cope with the flux of time. After all, the legal examples that I provided in Chapter 2, typifying the temporal problems, were eventually all "resolved" in the discussed legal cases. With Greenhouse, we could say that one of the functions of law is precisely to preserve certain indeterminacies of time, instead of solving them. The central tension that I have described in this book between temporal governance and human time is an example of an indeterminacy of time – of the Janus face of time if you wish – that should be preserved. Arguing that the value of human time should trump any other consideration would oversimplify the complexity of the role and meaning of legal time.

In legal time, often multiple competing interests and values are reflected and balanced. Countdown deadlines, for example, are temporal boundaries in which the limitation is linked to two dates by a precise quantity of time. Such countdown deadlines can be used as probationary time for long-term residence status, or naturalization as we have seen, yet they are also used as limitations for waiting. The point of such deadlines is, as Elizabeth Cohen argues, that they leave room for more normative complexity that will only increase after lapse of time. "Compared to having one's fate determined at birth, having a period of time in which claims may be staked leaves open the possibility for judgment, reasoning, and changes of circumstance," Cohen writes.[47] They acknowledge that in legal decision-making, compelling reasons often contradict one another. I would say that this normative complexity is not restricted to countdown deadlines but equally applies to other usage of legal time. Take for example the distinction between ex nunc and ex tunc that was at the heart of the case of Eritrean girl mentioned in Chapter 1. The possibility of assessing a case *as if* it is still the past or taking into account the actual developments after the initial decision leaves room for evaluating different interests, such as abuse of new procedures *versus* an effective remedy.

I argue, however, that this normative complexity should explicitly take into account the value of human time. The crux of the jus temporis that I present is that temporal governance finds its limitation in the value of human time: temporal governance should be balanced with the impact it has in terms of human time. The implication of this is that it should always be *possible* to end at a certain moment the exclusion from legal entitlements by means of time, and subsequently a point in time in which further temporal exclusion is simply *impossible*, legally speaking.

Of course, this immediately begs the question: *When* exactly should these two elements (the possibility to end the exclusion and the impossibility to pursue it) be operationalized? The point is that such a point in time should not merely be expressed in clock but also explicitly in human time. That is to say, of course any reference to lapse of time will inevitably make use of the clock. Yet, the focal point for operationalizing jus temporis should be the human time of the individual. Therefore, jus temporis should precisely address the characteristics of individual human time. This will not only enable account being taken into the normative value of human time that stems from its finite, irreversible, and unstoppable character, it will also provide the opportunity to evaluate the age, lifetime, and expectation of the particular migrant. Again, my argument is not meant to undermine or contradict prevailing arguments, grounds, or rules for inclusion and exclusion of migrants over time. Yet, next to the arguments that qualify the presence and behavior of

46 Greenhouse, "Just in Time." 47 Cohen, *The Political Value of Time*, p. 56.

a migrant (based on integration, ties, or otherwise), I discern an argument that is simply based on the value of the lapse of human time itself. The core of my argument is that the enduring exclusion of migrants that are present within the territory of (stronger) residence entitlements should be proportionate in relation to harm expressed in terms of the human time of the individual at stake. To be sure, with this I refer to *individual* human time and not time as proxy for something else, or to the passage of time that matter because of what that normally signifies about the development of a human life, as scholars like Carens argue. The meaning of lapsed time in the life of the particular individual should be taken into account as having value.

I would suggest that operationalizing jus temporis should consist of both a formal and a material criterion. The first limb as to the possibility to end the exclusion from residence entitlements would imply a proportionality assessment in which (next to other arguments and grounds) the value of human time should be explicitly weighed against the interest to pursue the exclusion. To be sure, this does not imply that we end up with precisely the material time criterion that I have criticized in the foregoing for being too meritocratic. The point here is not so much to provide a material assessment of ties, integration, assimilation, or whatever substantial criterion a country might have to assess eligibility for inclusion. A proportionality assessment of whether the length of a procedure is justified or whether the qualification as temporary or unlawful of long-term residence is deemed to be just cannot simply limit its reference to clock time. It must take into account the specific characteristics of the lapse of human time. It is not such much the evaluation of what has happened in a certain life, which is at stake, but the mere fact that this life has taken human time. In other words, the quality of time should not be measured but the lapse of human time as such.

Yet, the second limb of jus temporis should be expressed in a formal time criterion: no matter what is at stake in a certain procedure, or regarding the long-term residence of certain migrants, there should be a final limit to the possibility to prolong their exclusion. Then again, in such a formal criterion, a multitude of competing interests and values can be reflected and balanced. The exact term will therefore depend on different elements: the reasons and grounds for the exclusion; the weight a certain government attaches to exclusion (which will change over time); maybe the categories of migrants to whom it applies; the general hospitality toward strangers; and so on. I do not think that such a term can be provided in general for every situation, every country, and every time; I simple hold that the law should always provide for such a temporal limit to exclusion. A countdown criterion has as important quality – it ends a process that would otherwise continue indefinitely.

In the following, I discuss three pertinent issues that arise when jus temporis is at stake: the limit to waiting time in procedures; the length of time that long-term residence can remain temporary; and the issue of regularization of long-term unlawful residence. They all share the central tension of this book: the temporal governance of the process of someone's presence within the territory becomes increasingly strained with the lapse of human time. Moreover, in all three, equally demanding interests and values are at stake in the use of legal time that could not easily be mitigated.

Waiting Time

One of the prerogatives of the sovereign is that they never have to wait but are waited upon. As discussed in Chapter 1, waiting is not merely a by-product of migration law, it is an important means of temporal governance. Long waiting periods in asylum procedures, for example, or the time spent in immigration detention awaiting expulsion are both highly suited for temporal governance. The Procedures Directive,[48] for example, stipulates that asylum procedures should be concluded as soon as possible, and any case within six months. Member States may only extend the time limit of the procedure for a period not exceeding a further nine months if a case is very complex; there is a situation of high influx; or the applicant fails to live up to certain obligations to cooperate in the procedure. Moreover, the time limit may be extended due to an uncertain situation in the country of origin.[49] In any case, the maximum time limit is twenty-one months.[50] Similar limits to waiting time can be found in the rules regulating immigration detention. Detention for the purpose of removal according to Article 15 of the Returns Directive should be as short as possible, with a maximum of six months. When the migrant does not cooperate with removal or it is difficult to obtain the necessary documents, the period of detention may be extended another twelve months. As regards border detention, Article 9 of the Qualification Directive also stipulates that this should be as short as possible. Moreover, lawfulness of the detention should be reviewed at reasonable intervals of time. Another obvious example of waiting time is the period family members can be made to wait before they can reunite with their "sponsors" under the Family Reunification Directive (Article 8, Directive 2003/86).[51] In such cases, there is quite a large margin of appreciation for states to keep them waiting in order for the spouse to first integrate in the country, even though the CJEU has held that "a waiting period cannot be imposed without taking into account, in specific cases, all the relevant factors."[52]

Still, what is the rationale behind these procedural terms? Time of such a procedure or detention reflects the different, often mutually exclusive interests at stake. Take for example the waiting period of asylum procedures.[53] The Procedures Directive basically balances two equally demanding principles that dictate the length of the procedure: the need for a fast and simple procedure, and the necessity of a fair and effective procedure.[54] So, legally, asylum procedures should not take too long, nor should they be too quick, why?

48 Directive 2013/32/EU of the European Parliament and of the Council of June 26, 2013, on common procedures for granting and withdrawing international protection [2013] OJ L 180/60.

49 Article 31(4) RAPD

50 Article 31(5) RAPD. There is, however, quite some "temporal discretion" in asylum procedures to prolong the waiting time of asylum seekers, see Reneman and Stronks, "What Are They Waiting For?," pp. 319–25.

51 The rationale behind this period of time is that it would enable the sponsor to first integrate in the host country, "by ensuring that family reunification does not take place until the sponsor has found in the host State a solid base, both economic and domestic, for settling a family there." ECJ June 27, 2006, *Parliament* v. *Council*, C-540/03, paragraph 93.

52 Ibid., paragraph 99. The European Courts of Human Rights has concluded that "beyond two years the insurmountable obstacles to enjoying family life in the country of origin progressively assume more importance in the fair balance assessment." ECHR July 9, 2021, *M. A.* v. *Denmark*, 6697/18, paragraph 193. I would think that such a reasoning is also based on an evaluation of the human time of the family members within the scope of their family life under Article 8 ECHR, see similarly ECHR July 10, 2014, *Senigo Longue et Autres* v. *France*, 19113/09, paragraphs 69–75.

53 The following description of the principles behind procedural waiting is taken from an article that I wrote together with Reneman, "What Are They Waiting For?" – see for a more elaborate discussion of the instrumental use of acceleration and deceleration as forms of temporal governance and the relationship with law and temporal discretion.

54 COM(2011) 319 final.

Lengthy asylum procedures seem, at first sight, to violate EU law. According to EU law, it is in the interest of both asylum seekers and the EU Member States to decide as soon as possible on asylum applications.[55] After all, the refugee is in immediate need of protection, while the host country wants to return the rejected asylum seeker to their country of origin as soon as possible. Quick asylum procedures prevent the asylum seeker from being "kept in suspense for an unduly long period of time."[56] They are also in the interest of genuine refugees and persons in need of subsidiary protection because they "would enjoy quicker access to entitlements."[57] Additionally, speedy procedures foster "employability of refugees and persons in need of subsidiary protection, as their skills would suffer less from a long period without full access to the labour market."[58] For this reason, the Procedures Directive mentions explicitly that Member States may prioritize asylum cases that are likely to be well-founded.[59]

Endless procedures in which the asylum seeker has to *wait* for a final decision seem to benefit no one. Waiting is often perceived as a waste of time,[60] and for asylum seekers it constitutes an "in-between" situation, after which life "could then move forward."[61] Whereas this does not serve to say that the waiting time of asylum seekers necessarily equates lost or empty time, it often consists of long periods of *ennui* and inactivity.[62] And such waiting time, the experience of being stuck in seemingly endless waiting periods, combined with the unpredictability of the outcomes can have detrimental effects on well-being of these migrants.[63]

Moreover, high speed can be in the interest of the Member States.[64] The reason for this is that it reduces reception costs and promotes the return of failed asylum seekers.[65] Moreover, the European Commission thinks that it is reasonable that Member States deal with manifestly unfounded asylum cases in shorter procedures than in normal cases because they are less complex. Short procedures for such cases prevent abuse of the asylum procedure.[66] Asylum procedures may also be accelerated in the interest of national security or public order.[67]

Nevertheless, a procedure that is purely based on the principle "the sooner the better" would clearly lead to unjust results.[68] Therefore, the Procedures Directive and case-law *also* stress that time limits may not undermine the fairness of the asylum procedure.[69] It takes time to examine the applicant's statements and documents in order to reveal whether the

[55] Recital 18 Preamble and Article 23(2) RAPD.

[56] Proposal for a Council Directive on minimum standards on procedures in Member States for granting and withdrawing refugee status (2001/C 62 E/16), explanation Article 23.

[57] COM(2009) 554 final. [58] COM(2011) 319 final. [59] Article 31(7) RAPD.

[60] Eule et al., *Migrants before the Law*, p. 152; B. Schwartz, "Waiting, Exchange, and Power: The Distribution of Time in Social Systems," *American Journal of Sociology* 79, no. 4 (1974).

[61] R. Rotter, "Waiting in the Asylum Determination Process: Just an Empty Interlude," *Time and Society* 25, no. 1 (2016), p. 88.

[62] Griffiths, "Out of Time"; C. Kobelinski, *L'accueil des demandeurs d'asile: Une ethnographie de l'attente* (Paris: Éditions du Cygne, 2010), p. 147.

[63] A. Wyss, "Stuck in Mobility? Interrupted Journeys of Migrants with Precarious Legal Status in Europe," *Journal of Immigrant & Refugee Studies* 17, no. 1 (2019).

[64] Recital 18 Preamble RAPD. [65] COM(2016) 467 final. [66] Ibid. [67] Proposal RAPD 2011.

[68] J. Hambly and N. Gill, "Law and Speed: Asylum Appeals and the Techniques and Consequences of Legal Quickening," *Journal of Law and Society* 47, no. 1 (2020).

[69] Recital 18 Preamble and Article 31(2) RAPD, ECtHR February 2, 2012, 9152/09, *I. M.* v. *France*, CJEU January 31, 2013, *H. I. D*, C-175/11, paragraph 75.

asylum seeker legally is a refugee or an irregular migrant. Some cases simply need alot of time to investigate facts and evidence or are legally highly complex. The European Commission recognizes that speedy asylum procedures should not undermine the quality of asylum decisions, amongst others, because this may lead to more appeals and therefore longer procedures.[70] Short time limits should be accompanied by procedural safeguards for the asylum seeker, such as free legal aid.[71] Even though Member States may accelerate and prioritize the procedure in certain situations, the asylum seeker must enjoy a sufficient period of time within which to gather and present the necessary material in support of their application, thus allowing the determining authority to carry out a fair and comprehensive examination of those applications and to ensure that the applicants are not exposed to any dangers in their country of origin. [72]

The length of the asylum procedure is therefore shaped by the need for a fast and simple procedure *and* the necessity of a fair and effective procedure. Clearly, these principles can be at odds, especially if one takes into the equation that it is unreasonable to expect a government to spend all of its resources on one branch of government. Moreover, in practice it turns out that there is ample opportunity to let migrants wait, simply because there is still quite some flexibility in the legal framework to wait before the procedure commences or to prolong procedures; to prolong procedures according to the rules; or to simply let asylum seekers wait, even though there is no legitimate ground for this. And, even if there is no legitimate ground for such waiting, in the latter scenario, the asylum seeker would need to start a procedure to argue that the government broke the rules, and such a procedure takes more time.

There we have it, the complexity of interests behind the length of an asylum procedure makes it difficult to set general temporal limitations, yet I maintain that the waste of human time eventually finds its limitations in the value of jus temporis. I assert that the rationale behind the limitations that can be found in the Procedures Directive are – or should be – in the end, an expression of jus temporis, the value of human time. The countdown deadlines that are set to temper this form of temporal governance are meant to protect wasting human time.[73] It is in this sense that procedural terms are clear examples of temporal mechanisms that counter the endless possibilities of temporal governance. Yet, the friction between legal and human time becomes rather apparent in the starting time of the residence entitlement after a successful asylum application. Such a permit can be antedated to the moment of application, just as entitlements for family reunification can be attached to that moment, as seen with case of the Eritrean girl in Chapter 1. Such antedating might be a proper technique to deal with the problem that much time has lapsed since the moment of the application, therewith granting certain entitlements to the earlier moment. This same case, however, illustrated that despite the antedating, the lapse of human time could not be stopped. Just before her twenty-second birthday, it turned out that she was, legally speaking, seventeen years old.

[70] COM(2016) 467 final. [71] Ibid.

[72] CJEU January 31, 2013, *H. I. D.* and *B. A.* v. *Refugee Applications Commissioner and Others*, C-175/11.

[73] A similar reasoning could be detected as regards the waiting period for family reunification, the ECtHR concluded that whilst a waiting period of two years is acceptable as a requirement of integration, "it is of the view that beyond such duration the insurmountable obstacles to enjoying family life in the country of origin progressively assume more importance in the fair balance assessment." ECHR July 9, 2021, *M. A.* v. *Denmark*, 6697/18, paragraphs 162 and 193.

Yet, just as antedating cannot really turn back time, these countdown deadlines are in practice rather imperfect mechanisms for the protection of jus temporis. After all, if the government fails to meet these deadlines, it is the migrant who has to act by either starting a new procedure for damages for noncompliance or otherwise forcing the government to take a decision. I argue that starting a procedure for damages for noncompliance or otherwise forcing the government to take action serves as the aforementioned *possibility* to limit temporal governance based on jus temporis.

However, precisely because the government's inaction in such scenarios is itself a form of temporal governance, which costs human time, I claim that there should eventually also be an *impossibility* of further wasting human time. A stronger form of protection is therefore a countdown deadline, which when expired, leads to automatically granting the initial request. In the Netherlands, such a policy existed for years, called the "three-year policy," which stipulated that if the government had not taken a decision on the application for a residence permit, and the migrant had not deliberately decelerated the procedure, this would lead to an automatic residence permit. In the Dublin Regulation, such mechanisms also exists, for example, albeit without immediately leading to a residence status. If a Member State does not respond within a short period of time to a request to take back an asylum seeker as per the relevant regulation, this leads to an obligation to take back the person concerned (Article 25 Regulation 604/2013). Such a countdown deadline provides a better protection of jus temporis and an incentive for the government to accelerate procedures and not deliberately waste human time.

The normative limitation jus temporis sets to delimit the sovereign prerogative to let migrants wait is founded in the value of human time, and implies two concrete temporal mechanisms. First, there should be the *possibility* to force the government to take action and stop migrants from waiting any longer on the outcome of their procedure, an example of which is a procedure for damages for noncompliance. Secondl there should be the mere *impossibility* to extend the waste of time after a certain amount of human time, by simply providing the migrant a residence entitlement based on the government's inaction.

When Does Temporariness End?

The relationship between legal and human time is difficult to grasp, as we have seen. Again, as easy as it is to say that procedures may not take *too long*, that the legitimacy of detention should be reviewed *as soon as possible*, or that a migrant should be able to apply for naturalization at a *reasonable* moment in time; as difficult it is to conclude in a specific case *when* exactly it took *too* long or *when* something is as soon as possible or at a reasonable moment. One of the main advantages of clock time – that it refers to processes without exactly pinpointing it – is precisely what makes it so apt for temporal governance, and what makes it so difficult to pinpoint the exact moment that the lapse of time becomes unjust. Still, I argue that there is a point in time when temporal governance becomes unjust, and this also applies to the question of how long residence can be qualified as "temporary."

Clearly, temporal differentiation based on "temporariness" is one of the main features of contemporary practices of exclusion in European law and policy. Not only are some forms of (long-term) residence categorized as "temporary," temporal exclusion could just as well take place after migrants have naturalized. In other words, temporariness is not restricted to residence status but often also linked to identity. As Halleh Ghorashi has argued in line with the work of Malkki, the said "sedentary bias" is used in integration discourse to argue that certain citizens still belong to their "country of origin" more than to their new home country.[74] In such a sense, temporariness is being detached from actual lapse of human time; something that becomes most obvious in terms such as "second or third generation migrant." Such "migrants" have in fact never migrated, they have spent their entire life in the same country, still their residence status and/or identity remains "temporary." One could dub this a form of eternal temporariness, in which time is clearly used as a moving image of eternity in which there is no room for actual change.

Despite such practices of exclusion, I would argue that limitations of such temporal governance regarding the residence entitlements of migrants are to be found in jus temporis. Even though European migration law bears witness to the possibilities of temporal differentiation by means of "temporality," one can just as well find traces of the limitations to such practices. However, in order to be able to identify these elements of jus temporis, it is first of all important to distinguish between "temporariness" as existing legal category and de facto "temporariness." As seen in Chapter 1, the former is reserved in European law for certain categories of migrants whose residence goal is deemed to be temporary: students; *au pairs*; seasonal workers. For such residence permits, the end date is foreseen at the moment when the entitlement is granted, often directly linked to certain activities within the territory.[75] After this period, the migrant might leave the territory or request a new residence title. This legal temporariness should be distinguished from de facto temporariness, for the latter signifies all forms of residence entitlements that can be withdrawn or could otherwise lead to the forced expulsion of the person concerned. In this sense, legal temporariness consists of de facto temporariness, for its end is legally foreseen at the moment that the status is granted, yet de facto *temporariness* is a broader concept. To be able to identity the latter, it is useful to seek its counterpart.

Legally speaking, "nationality" is the status that, in general, provides the safety of permanence, even though the revocation of citizenship has a long history.[76] Formally, nationality has been defined as the legal bond between a person and a state, a definition that can also be found for example in Article 2(a) of the European Convention on Nationality. Although this Council of Europe convention is not signed and ratified by all European countries, it is certainly one of the most authoritative European documents regarding nationality.[77] The definition refers to the famous *Nottebohm* case of the International Court of Justice, in which the concept of nationality was explored for the first time. This court defined nationality as "a legal bond having as its basis a social fact of

[74] Ghorashi, "Negotiating Belonging beyond Rootedness."

[75] In the Migration Law Clinic expert opinion, five elements are identified that make residence "temporary by its very nature": the short and regulated duration of the residence right; the factual impossibility to prolong such a residence right for successive periods, including beyond a five-year period; the non-continuous nature of the residence; the retention of a principal residence elsewhere; and the limited purpose of the residence, based on a certain activity that is limited in time, see Vrije Universiteit Amsterdam Migration Law Expert Opinion, "Assessing the Temporariness of the Chavez-Vilchez Right of Residence," April 2021, available at https://migrationlawclinic.org/2021/04/23/assessing-the-temporariness-of-the-chavez-vilchez-right-of-residence/.

[76] M. J. Gibney, "Should Citizenship Be Conditional? The Ethics of Denationalization," *The Journal of Politics* 75, no. 3 (2013).

[77] L. Pilgram, "International Law and European Nationality Laws," *EUDO Citizenship Policy Brief* (2011), https://cadmus.eui.eu/bitstream/handle/1814/19455/EUDO_CIT_2011_01_Pilgram.pdf?sequence=1.

attachment, a genuine connection of existence, interests and sentiments, together with the existence of reciprocal rights and duties."[78] If nationality is acquired, it is generally very difficult to lose it again. A state party, as a general rule in the European Convention on Nationality, may not provide in its internal law for the removal of nationality of one of its nationals, except in certain limited cases (Article 7, paragraph 1). Among these cases are most notably: (1) the voluntary acquisition of another nationality; (2) if the nationality is acquired by means of fraudulent conduct; (3) voluntary service in a foreign military force; (4) conduct seriously prejudicial to the vital interests of the state party; and (5) lack of a genuine link between the state party and a national habitually residing abroad. There is, however, another limitation that better reflects the very exceptional character of the loss of nationality. A state may not provide for the loss of nationality if this implies that the person concerned becomes stateless as a result. As a general rule, only if a person holds a second nationality is it possible to lose nationality.

So, we could conclude that, generally, the acquisition of nationality takes away the temporary character – defined as the possibility to be forced to leave the territory – of residence. What then is the relationship between the acquisition of nationality and lapse of time? Again, the European Convention on Nationality provides an important indication. In Article 6, paragraph 3, it is stated that a nationality procedure should be available for "persons lawfully and habitually residing on its territory. In establishing the conditions for naturalization, it shall not provide for a period of residence exceeding ten years before the lodging of an application." The explanatory report of the Convention stresses that this provision in fact reflects a common European standard, most European countries already required a period of between five and ten years of residence.[79] In other words, European countries, in practice, use a countdown deadline for acquiring a status that is no longer temporary. I would say that this is, along with other arguments for inclusion, also an acknowledgment of jus temporis: countries provide the opportunity to apply for permanent residence status after time – indirectly acknowledging the problematic character of keeping someone permanently at risk of losing their residence status.

However, the possibility of acquiring nationality clearly does not equate with granting nationality. European law does not consist of an automatic award of citizenship after a lapse of time, as argued for by Rubio-Marín. It is perfectly conceivable that such a request could be denied, for example, because the migrant does not meet integration criteria, or has a criminal record. Moreover, for all kinds of reasons, migrants sometimes choose not to naturalize, or simply do not qualify for it. The case of Len van Heest discussed in the previous paragraph exemplifies the possibility of long-term residence that remains de facto "temporary." As I argued, it is the case of these long-term residing migrants that breach public order that best demonstrate the case of jus temporis. The more human time has lapsed in uncertainty, the more temporal governance risks becoming unjust. But when?

I consider that temporal governance becomes unjust if it does not provide for rules that first entail the *possibility* of acquiring permanent status (albeit long-term residence or citizenship); and second, the *impossibility* of losing that status at a certain moment in time. In other words, in addition to a countdown deadline for the acquisition of nationality, I would argue for an end term for the termination of long-term residence on any ground.

[78] ICJ April 6, 1955, *Nottebohm* case, ICJ Reports 1955, p. 23.

[79] Council of Europe, *European Convention on Nationality: Explanatory Report* (Strasbourg: Council of Europe, 1997), p. 9.

After such an end term, temporary residence becomes automatically permanent. To use the Netherlands again as an example, until 2012, a procedural end term was in force that prohibited the withdrawal of long-term residence in cases of breach of public order. After twenty years of lawful residence, the possibility of residency withdrawal for reasons of public order expired. Clearly, this would leave the possibility of expelling migrants before the end term in force, thus acknowledging the competing interests of individuals and society at work in such an assessment. Yet, the value of human time would after such a period of time simply prevail. To put it differently, it acknowledges the actual human time that has lapsed, which is finite and irreversible, by acknowledging that the status has become de facto permanent.

To be sure, I do not propose in general that such an impossibility should be fixed at twenty years of residence. I simply argue that, normatively speaking, there should be a point in time after which the migrant's residence can legally no longer be held to be temporary. The basis for such a point in time should be human time.

Regularization

One of the most controversial figures of contemporary migration law is the regularization or amnesty of long-term residing undocumented migrants.[80] I claim that a regularization endeavors to mediate the complex interplay between the legal order and individual time of the migrant. In a regularization, migrants who have resided within the territory for a certain period of time get the chance to regularize their migration status based on their mere presence. Amnesty for immigrants implies a kind of "legal alchemy," as Linda Bosniak puts it, "through such policies, the irregular is made regular, the unlawful lawful."[81] And it is precisely this alchemy that leads to so much controversy: for some, a regularization constitutes the paradigmatic example of a policy that rewards lawbreakers and even incentivizes further lawbreaking, yet for others, it is the fulfillment of nothing less than restorative justice. Ayelet Shachar equally observes that this debate is at stalemate. On the one side she discerns the "nation-of-laws camp" that maintains that people who have breached the country's immigration laws by entering without permission can never overcome this "original sin." On the other side of the debate, she finds the "nation-of-immigrants perspective," stressing that "if America is to remain an open and welcoming nation, it must create a path for undocumented migrants to emerge from the shadows and gain legal status as part of a comprehensive – and humane – immigration reform project."[82] These positions are irreconcilable, she holds, because an emphasis on compassion and human dignity is unlikely to convince the hardline restrictionists that make up a section of the nation-of-laws.

[80] I will use amnesty, regularization, and pardon as synonyms here, for differences in meaning see L. Bosniak, "Amnesty in Immigration: Forgetting, Forgiving, Freedom," *Critical Review of International Social and Political Philosophy* 16, no. 3 (2013). Ricoeur claims that a pardon can only be provided for by the victim in cases of criminal or historic injustices, see P. Ricoeur, *The Just* (Chicago: The University of Chicago Press, 2000), pp. 143–5. Clearly, such an analogy with regularization in the sphere of migration does not hold water, for there is no clear victim to the transgression of migration laws.

[81] Bosniak, "Amnesty in Immigration," p. 344.

[82] Shachar, "Earned Citizenship," p. 113.

Shachar argues that those who are against regularization often complain that the migrants "original sin" of breaking the immigration laws should not be forgotten.[83] The initial decision of exclusion, in other words, should be frozen in time and keep its force.[84] Such argument should not be ridiculed since, after all, as a starting point, conformity is essential for every legal rule to function properly: if it does not matter whether one obeys a certain rule in practice, the said rule loses effect. Or as David Miller puts it specifically regarding regularizations in immigration cases: "[t]he integrity of the system would be put in question if amnesties were simply granted unconditionally."[85] A system of migration rules that intends to regulate the inclusion and exclusion of migrants within a territory but does not effectuate the removal of migrants from its territory clearly has no effect. This presumption is evidently at the basis of the EU Returns Directive, which creates common standards and procedures between Member States of the EU for returning illegally residing migrants. Recital 4 of the Directive stipulates that "clear, transparent and fair rules need to be fixed to provide for an effective return policy as a necessary element of a well-managed migration policy." This is the obvious aim of the Return Directive and highlights that a "well managed migration policy" has in addition to its rules regulating entry and stay, regulations for the return of migrants. And migrants that simply stay within the territory therefore undermine this starting point. Exclusion is the inevitable counterpart of inclusion, as the control over the presence in the territory both implies rules regulating entry, stay, and return.

How does such exclusion relate to time then? It is one thing that someone is removed from the territory at a certain moment, yet if this means that the migrant immediately reenters the territory, this exclusion has no durable effect. Hence, avoiding such immediate return of unwanted migrants is the rationale behind entry bans, which could be understood as countdown deadlines that freeze the legal effect or force of the decision to remove someone from the territory in time. The Return Directive stipulates as general rule that an entry ban should not exceed five years. Whilst this entry ban demonstrates the attempt to durably effectuate the removal decision, it similarly shows that the duration of such exclusion is limited in time. In other words, as common as it is to freeze the effect of a decision in time – to provide it a durable force or effect – as usual it is to limit the duration of such "freezing" in clock time.

Could we then say that the argument of the "original sin" could equally be frozen in clock time – or to put it differently, is there a legal or normative limitation to the state's

[83] Bosniak has criticized the claim that migrants have committed at least a pro tanto wrong against the state, thereby furthering the interiorization of the border, L. Bosniak, "Wrongs, Rights and Regularization," *Moral Philosophy and Politics* 3, no. 2 (2016). I take the "original sin argument" here simply as existing in the debate about regularization and merely ask how it relates to (human) time. It is tempting to elaborate here on theological connotations in the meaning of "original sin," and the question of how this relate to human time. Can human kind overcome the "original sin" of consuming the forbidden fruit? In many different ways this formulation is highly problematic, which for reasons of time and space in this text, I have to leave aside here.

[84] One could argue that it is not so much an "original sin" but a repetition of "sins," after all, the presence of the migrant in the territory remains unlawful, so they constantly break the laws of entry. Interestingly enough, this discussion coincides with theological discussions as to the meaning of the "original sin" and the expulsion from Paradise, as either a one-time sin, or as installing in human nature the ability to sin and responsibility for all subsequent sins, see G. Agamben, *The Kingdom and the Garden* (London: Seagull Books, 2020).

[85] Miller, *Strangers in Our Midst*, p. 126.

capacity to uphold the initial decision to refuse lawful residence?[86] To answer this question, it is important to emphasize that regularization only arises for those who have not departed or have been removed from the territory. This in itself is for some yet another argument against regularization, for it would be unjust for those who did obey the rules. Moreover, some consider regularization as an incentive for going into hiding, or even as an incentive to live in deplorable circumstances for years. Still, the unlawful presence of migrants is not permitted, and legally speaking the state has every right to expel them as long as they are on the territory. Article 6 (1) of the Returns Directive stipulates that Member States can issue a decision to return the migrant who stays illegally on their territory. Such a return decision is an administrative or judicial decision to declare the stay of a migrant to be illegal and impose an obligation to return. The moment the stay of a migrant ceases to be legal, a return decision is issued and they are under an obligation to return. It is this obligation to leave the territory that is the pivot on which the Return Directive turns. The failure to remove a migrant from the territory does not erode this obligation to leave. There is no legal deadline for this provision in the Returns Directive. Still, the residence remains unlawful over time, and long-term, unlawfully residing migrants also illustrate the state's inability to effectuate its own rules in practice. Even though the legal obligation to leave the territory remains in force, and the state has the right to effectuate this, de facto some migrants still remain present within the territory over time.

So how should we evaluate this durable exclusion of residence entitlements for those who remain present within the territory? On the one hand, it is obvious that the unlawfully residing migrant is obliged to leave the territory and that such an obligation is not eroded over time. On the other hand, there is the de facto situation that some migrants do reside long-term within a territory. Shachar argues that their de facto social membership should retrospectively be acknowledged, as we have seen. To avoid the said stalemate, Shachar introduces jus nexi, in which one retrospectively acknowledges the actual community membership that the migrant has de facto established over time. Time clearly has an important role to play in this claim: it is the acknowledgment of the membership that has developed during the actual time that the migrant has lived within the territory. Yet, as argued in the previous paragraph, whilst such argument makes use of the temporality of human time, retrospectively focussing on the becoming rooted of the migrant, it does not expose the full argumentative force of human time in law. As demonstrated with the case of Len van Heest, the fifty-seven years he spent in Canada are not simply a proxy for a process that has developed; nor were these objective years, these fifty-seven years were *his* years, it was *his* time; finite and irreversible as they elapsed. Human time itself has value, that is the crux of the matter. Hence, the claim for rootedness over time gains weight when it does not silently equate time with lapse of clock time, as proxy for something else, but attaches proper weight to the meaning of human time. I would argue that this element of rootedness

[86] There is ample philosophical literature on the meaning of the pardon and its relationship with the question of time, see e.g. J. Derrida, *Pardonner: L'impardonnable et l'imprescriptible* (Paris: Éditions Galilée, 2012); J. Derrida, *Le Parjure et le pardon*, Volume 1: Séminaire (1997–1998) (Paris: Éditions du Seuil, 2019); S. Guerlac, "The Fragility of the Pardon (Derrida and Ricoeur)," in *Derrida and the Time of the Political*, eds. P. Cheah and S. Guerlac (Durham, NC: Duke University Press, 2009), pp. 255–73; Ost, *Le Temps du Droit*, pp. 111–57; Ricoeur, *Memory, History, Forgetting*, pp. 457–500. This body of literature, however, deals with historical injustice or very serious criminal offenses or even crimes against humanity, and the relationship between the offender, the victim, and society.

based on human time plays a role in any claim for regularization, *in addition to* more meritocratic arguments based on ties or egalitarian arguments based on citizenship.

In addition to this argument of social inclusion, Shachar has argued that an appeal to the legal concept of "adverse possession" should be taken into consideration when evaluating the question of whether unlawful residence should lead to a form of regularization.[87] The analogy is with property that has been acquired without the consent of the owner and kept in possession over a long period of time whilst the owner does not take steps to recover their property. In the words of David Miller "Thus the doctrine of adverse possessions brings together the possessors' reasonable expectation that she can continue to hold and use what she has been holding and using over a long stretch of time and the previous owner's indifference toward (or, it might be said, implicit consent to) his loss of property."[88] Even though Miller questions whether the analogy has much value in cases in which unlawfully residing migrants try to remain invisible, he agrees with Shachar that when the government turns a blind eye to their presence, they have a very strong case for regularization.[89]

Another way of approaching the conundrum of the persistent legal exclusion of de facto long-term, unlawfully residing migrants is by raising the question of whether the state can – normatively speaking – simply ignore the durable presence of the migrant since the initial decision to refuse lawful entry, whilst it in the meantime has not succeeded in expelling the migrant. Given the fact that the obligation to leave the territory does not erode over time, and when focussing on the situation in which the migrant purposely evades the governmental eye, simply in order to remain within the territory, does one ever reach a moment in time in which the permanent exclusion of these present migrants becomes unjust? Or, let me stretch this question to its threshold, can the state exclude someone from residence entitlements – while they remain present within the territory – *forever*?

With this formulation we are back at the discussion of the difference between eternity and mortality in Chapter 2. It seems as if in the argument of the "original sin," an eternal conception of time is at work, an immovable time that remains untouched by the changing character of human time. Such "eternal" exclusion, without prospect of inclusion, without at least a periodic evaluation, is at odds with the normative characteristics of jus temporis because it does not take into account human time. In the practice of European migration law, such a form of "eternal exclusion" might not exist: migration law has ample opportunities to regularize one's stay, for example, by an Article 8 claim, or based on a new application for medical reasons, or a proportionality assessment. I hold that such mechanisms precisely express jus temporis – the *possibility* to regularize once exclusion at a certain point in time. Still, the question remains what the normative argument behind this is, precluding an eternal form of exclusion.

[87] Shachar, *The Birthright Lottery*, pp. 184–8. [88] Miller, *Strangers in Our Midst*, p. 122.

[89] The ECtHR also acknowledges this in its case-law, see e.g. EHRM June 30, 2015, *A. S. v. Switzerland*, 39350/13, where the Court recalls in paragraph 44

> that where a Contracting State tolerates the presence of an alien in its territory, thereby allowing him or her to await a decision on an application for a residence permit, an appeal against such a decision or a fresh application for a residence permit, such a Contracting State enables the alien to take part in the host country's society, to form relationships and to create a family there. However, this does not automatically entail that the authorities of the Contracting State concerned are, as a result, under an obligation pursuant to Article 8 of the Convention to allow him or her to settle in their country.

As we have seen in the cases of *K.* and *H. F.* – 1Fers who are exempted from refugee protection because they allegedly committed a crime against peace, a war crime, or a crime against humanity – even in such cases there should be an assessment from time to time to establish whether an actual threat for public order still exists. Eternal exclusion cannot be put in terms of human time, at least not in general terms, for it would be entirely dependent on the lifetime of the individual at stake. This would imply that the measure would have a different effect merely depending on the lifespan of the individual, which in itself raises questions of proportionality. Freezing the "original sin" of trespassing migration rules forever, thereby excluding the unlawfully residing migrant eternally, without at least the possibility of regularizing the migrant's status, is unjust. In such a scenario, human time is fully replaced by an eternal conception of time, a moving image of eternity.

So, a regularization has to preserve the "integrity of the legal system" while simultaneously taking into account that eternal exclusion of unlawfully residing migrant is unjust. The tension between individual lifetime and the time of the social order needs to be mediated by at least providing for the *possibility* of inclusion and allowing for legal venues to at least apply for a form of amnesty or regularization after a lapse of time. This argument against eternal exclusion is closely related to the aforementioned argument of rootedness, which grants value to the mere lapse of human time.

A regularization, I would claim, creates a caesura, a break with the past.[90] In so doing, as Suzanne Guerlac explains while discussing the figure of the pardon in the work of Paul Ricoeur, Jacques Derrida, and Hannah Arendt, the pardon unbinds the present from the past. Importantly, this does not mean that the past action is forgotten, or that retrospectively the transgression is no longer condemned. "The act survives and remains condemned, but it survives *in the past*."[91] That is the "alchemy" of a regularization, it remembers the transgression but situates it in the past in order to stop the process of illegality and start anew.[92]

Instead of being at odds with a well-functioning system of migration law (because it would reward lawbreakers, or encourage people to go into hiding), I would say that it

90 Alexandre Lefebvre has argued that the strain between time and law becomes clear in its uneasy relationship with the role of "creativity" in legal judgments. Reading the legal realist Wendell Holmes with this Bergsonian criticism of time in mind, Lefebvre argues that it is precisely the role of adjudication to align the legal rules with the ever-going flux of time. "Judgements for Holmes, likes species and organisms for Bergson, are kinds of solutions to problems," Lefebvre contends. After all, rules always risk becoming meaningless over time, simply because the "interests and needs of a society are in a constant and continued flux," A. Lefebvre, "The Time of Law: Evolution in Holmes and Bergson," in *Deleuze and Law: Forensic Futures*, eds. R. Braidotti, C. Colebrook, and P. Hanafin (London: Palgrave Macmillan, 2009), pp. 37–42. I claim that something similar applies to the legal technique of regularization, which unbinds the past action from the present, therewith opening up a new future.

91 Guerlac, "The Fragility of the Pardon (Derrida and Ricoeur)," p. 270. This is, according to Ricoeur, the difference between amnesty – as it is etymologically related to amnesia – and pardon, the former is based on forgetting, the latter on a remembering of an act that is by means of the act of pardoning situated in the past. Ricoeur, *The Just*, pp. 143–5.

92 "The miracle that saves the world, the realm of human affairs, from its normal, 'natural' ruin is ultimately the fact of natality, in which the faculty of action is ontologically rooted. It is, in other words, the birth of new men and the new beginning, the action they are capable of by virtue of being born." H Arendt, *The Human Condition* (Chicago: The University of Chicago Press, 1998), p. 247. See also A. Gündogdu, *Rightlessness in an Age of Rights: Hannah Arendt and the Contemporary Struggles of Migrants* (Oxford: Oxford University Press, 2015), pp. 131–2.

precisely reflects the normative complexity of the situation of unlawfully residing migrants. It acknowledges retrospectively the de facto presence of the migrant over time; the value of rootedness as the lapse of irreversible and finite human time; the unjust character of eternal exclusion; and the legal necessity to update the law from time to time. In the meantime, however, the integrity of the system of migration control remains uneroded. After all, the obligation to follow the rules remains unaltered, only in exceptional circumstances and after the lapse of individual, finite human time *can* migrants be included. For that is the crux, the rules still apply for future cases, yet the regularization takes into account that in certain complex cases, the situation has changed because of the de facto presence and the human time that has lapsed ever since the initial decision to refuse entry. In such a situation, the transgression of the rules for entry in the particular case are being forgiven, therewith providing these migrants a future within the territory.

Again, I would argue that there should at least be a *possibility* for a regularization in law, which in fact already exists in many different manifestations. The most obvious example is to apply for a residence permit on the basis of an Article 8 ECHR claim. Even though the chances are not very high if one solely focuses on the case-law of the Court in cases of unlawfully residing migrants,[93] clearly such a legal pathway qualifies as a possibility for regularization. Other possibilities are residence permits on the basis of humanitarian grounds, for example, the German *Härtefallkommissionen*, a commission of citizens who make use of discretionary power to provide a residence status in exceptional humanitarian cases of long-term unlawfully residing migrants.[94]

In addition to this, I contend that there should be an *impossibility* to further exclude the migrant, after which someone's residence should in any case be regularized. This might be conceived as a rather far-fetched policy proposal, given the current strong sentiments against the regularization of unlawful presence of migrants in Europe. It is clear that durable presence is in many European countries nowadays not a guarantee for inclusion after time. It is in this sense that time has no progressive character for these migrants, as Honig, Anderson, and McNevin convincingly argue. It is rather the opposite, it is perfectly conceivable that people are excluded by means of time, even *forever*. Yet, as I have argued in this chapter, normatively speaking, the right of human time limits such forms of permanent exclusion. And just as time is apt for exclusion, it is perfectly fit for operationalizing inclusion on the basis of the normative value of human time in law.[95] I would argue that the impossibility to further exclude the migrant from lawful residence should be operationalized by means of a recurrent deadline after which it is examined which long-term residing migrant qualifies for regularization. Most countries do not use regularizations as recurrent deadlines, with a few exceptions.[96] Yet, such regularizations often return with a certain

[93] See e.g. EHRM April 26, 2007, *Konstantinov* v. *the Netherlands*, 16351/03; ECHR April 8, 2008, *Nnyanzi* v. *the United Kingdom*, 21878/08; ECHR June 28, 2011, *Nunez* v. *Norway*, 55597/09; ECHR February 14, 2012, *Antwi* v. *Norway*, 26940/10; ECHR December 4, 2012, *Butt* v. *Norway*, 47017/09; EHRM July 28, 2020, *Pormess* v. *the Netherlands*, 25402/14.

[94] E.g. www.innenministerium.bayern.de/mui/aufenthaltsrecht/haertefallkommission/index.php.

[95] In philosophical literature on the foundation of a pardon, it is suggested that a pardon is per its definition an extralegal category, I would think that at least the operationalization of the regularization that I propose here could certainly be put in legal rules and regulations. Ost, *Le Temps du Droit*, p. 138; Ricoeur, *The Just*, pp. 143–4.

[96] Whereas Northern European countries are more restrictive as regards regularization schemes for unlawful residence, Southern European countries are more often willing to regularize, see e.g.

rhythm, even when they have no permanent legal character. Regularization can be accompanied with a single-moment deadline, often to emphasize their nonrecurring character. Permanent regularizations have no single-moment deadline but instead make use of countdown deadlines relating to the length of residence, such regularizations are implemented on an on-going basis. Recurrent deadlines have strong normative legitimization, Cohen argues, because they are more democratically structured when "they are built using multiple points in time rather than single dates."[97] Moreover, the normative value of a regularization is that it has the ability to stop processes that would otherwise endure endlessly. Even though such regularization would be operationalized in terms of clock time, it would be founded on the human time that the migrant has spent, finite, irreversible, and unstoppable, and such time is one of the most precious "things" a human being possesses.

Conclusion: The Vanity of Legal Time

The painting on the cover of this book is from the Dutch seventeenth-century painter Pieter Claesz and is a vanitas painting, a subgenre of still life paintings that was rather popular at that time. In such paintings, the transience of earthly life is central, they present the edifying message that human time is relative to the coming eternal life. Vanity of vanities, all is vanity (*Vanitas vanitatum, et omnia vanitas*), as Ecclesiastes 1:2 has it. Four attributes in Claesz's painting function as a mnemonic device to remind the spectator of the transience of life: the skull, the tumbled glass, a timepiece that needs to be wound up, and an oil lamp that has just gone out. These items refer to man's mortality, just as decaying flowers, exuberant food dishes, and soap bubbles are often used for such purposes. The transience of human knowledge is depicted by a book, a goose quill, and some pieces of parchment, everything to acknowledge the vanity of human life. Clearly the vanitas painting fitted the dominant Calvinist morality of the day in the Netherlands. The spectator was warned not to forget that the earthly amusement is not everlasting, pursuing meaningless things is chasing after the wind.

As part of the *memento mori* tradition, the purpose of vanitas paintings was to list and specify worldly vices as a constant reminder for the pious Christian to avoid the sinful temptations of this life.[98] What can we take from this art tradition in the assessment of the role of legal time in the governance of migrants? What then is the vanity of legal time? The punchline of this book is rather simple: a conception of legal time that neglects or forgets the meaning and value of human time is vain. If legal time disregards the finite, irreversible, and unstoppable character of human time, it risks becoming unjust. The jus temporis that I have argued for in this chapter precisely aims to explicate this value of human time. Time spent within a territory matters, not only because it functions as a probationary period, reflecting different and competing conceptions of what is needed to allow inclusion into

A. Levinson, *The Regularisation of Unauthorized Migrants: Literature Survey and Country Case Studies* (Oxford: COMPAS, 2005), www.compas.ox.ac.uk/2005/er-2005-regularisation_unauthorized_literature/; W. Maas, "Unauthorized Migration and the Politics of Regularization, Legalization, and Amnesty," in *Labour Migration in Europe*, eds. G. Menz and A. Caviedes (London: Palgrave Macmillan, 2010).

97 Cohen, *The Political Value of Time*.

98 R. B. Sonnema, *The Early Dutch Vanitas Still-Life* (Michigan: University Microfilms Internationals, 1980), p. 109.

citizenry. Not just because of the qualification of the appropriate time, or because of the ties that have developed or the affiliations that have grown. Human time itself has value and should not be wasted.

Yet, it is important to emphasize that the virtues of legal time should not be ridiculed. As we have seen in Chapter 1, by means of an intricate usage of both clock and human time, all sorts of techniques of temporal differentiation are used to govern the presence of migrants within a territory. Time proves to be an utterly useful technique to make legal distinctions, no matter whether they are used to exclude or include migrants from legal entitlements. Moreover, one of the central qualities of legal time is that it refers both to eternal as well as finite, to general and individual, formal and material understandings of time.

Yet, it is this value of human time that I have endeavored to illuminate in the definition of rootedness that I proposed in this chapter. In order to make the value of human time as explicit as possible and to distinguish it from more meritocratic conceptions of temporal inclusion, such as ius nexi, I proposed to discern rootedness from integration. The latter signifying qualified time, the former mere lapse of human time. Rootedness simply signifies the entanglement of presence on a territory with the lapse of finite and irreversible human time. This conception of rootedness is consequently at the heart of jus temporis and its implications are not limited to questions of citizenship acquisition.

I have argued that the value of rootedness equally applies to waiting time in procedures, endless forms of temporariness, and unlawful residence. Concretely, I argue that this jus temporis implies two elements, no matter whether it is applied to waiting time, temporariness, or unlawful residence. The first is a certain openness to the future, the *possibility* that a certain situation will not last forever. In other words, the acknowledgment that time is not a moving image of eternity, but the lapse of time changes circumstances. For example, long-term migrants should be able to apply for long-term residence, or naturalization, or the lawfulness of detention should at least be reviewed from time to time. The second element is that there should be end terms at work in law, stipulating that a process needs to come to an end. Procedures may simply not last forever, temporariness may not continue eternally and there should be a moment when unlawful residences becomes lawful. Forgetting the normative value of human time, that is the vanity of legal time.

Conclusion

The Critical State of Jus Temporis in European Migration Law

> Summing up, we may say: time is Dasein.
>
> Martin Heidegger, *The Concept of Time*, 1924 AD

> Time is the substance of which I am made. Time is a river that sweeps me along, but I am the river; it is a tiger that mangles me, but I am the tiger; it is a fire that consumes me, but I am the fire.
>
> Jorge Luis Borges, *A New Refutation of Time*, 1947 AD

The refugee camp Moria on the Greek island Lesvos burned down in the week that I started writing this conclusion. The 12,500 asylum seekers who lived in the camp – designed for less than 3,000 inhabitants – were left sleeping rough and with little access to essential services, such as water, food supplies, and medical care. Amnesty International reported a drastic deterioration of the living conditions of asylum seekers in the Aegean Islands, with a disconcerting 30,000 living in various overcrowded facilities. Lesvos and Samos host currently more than four to eight times their respective capacities.

The Moria camp has been part of the European Hotspot Approach, which was launched in May 2015 in the European Agenda on Migration, as the EU's main response to the increased number of migrants arriving by sea. The approach consists of an infrastructure of detention in order to ensure swift identification, registration, and fingerprinting of migrants.[1] The hotspots are examples of "temporal borders," as Martina Tazzioli has argued, the border itself being one of the elements of temporal management.[2] Mobility is being disciplined by means of dates and deadlines, and importantly the differentiation in speed between different categories of migrants. The rapid identification, registration, and selection of asylum seekers upon landing is meant to differentiate the speed of the procedure and function as a "practice that ends up in slowing down the speed of some migrants' movements – generating protracted situations of legal limbo or preventively illegalizing asylum seekers – while hastening some others, as it is the case of deportations from Greece to Turkey and channels of expulsions."[3]

Tazzioli shows that by means of acceleration and deceleration, the possibilities for entering the asylum procedure and leaving the hotspots is drastically limited. Moreover, an important element of this policy is the constant alteration of the rules and deadlines regulating the temporal borders: the effect of which is confusion and uncertainty that, in

[1] B. Kasparek, "Routes, Corridors, and Spaces of Exception: Governing Migration and Europe," *Near Futures Online 1 "Europe at a Crossroads,"* (2016), http://nearfuturesonline.org/routes-corridors-and-spaces-of-exception-governing-migration-and-europe/.

[2] Tazzioli, "The Temporal Borders of Asylum." [3] Ibid., p. 18.

itself, produces effects of temporal suspension and spatial confinement of migrants. The temporal border adds a sense of existential immobility to the physical border, which Ghassan Hage has called "stuckedness."[4] Existential immobility is not limited to physical immobility – the impossibility to move from one location to another – rather, it is temporal, it is about whether one can move forward to a viable future. Stuckedness involves waiting, yet it is a hopeless sort of waiting. It is, as Anne McNevin succinctly captures it, "the combination of aspiration and the feeling of going nowhere, geographically, socially, or economically, in a world in which others are perceived as being unfairly and disproportionately mobile."[5] "Chronic waiting" is the effect of these temporal techniques of border control, implying long-term exclusion from geographic and social mobility.[6]

Such a sense of stuckedness is clearly one of the effects of temporal borders and is an important element of what Ayelet Shachar has called the "shifting border": the development that the gates no longer stand fixed at the country's territorial edges but that the border itself has become a moving construct, both spatially as well as temporal.

> Just as the shifting border extends the long arm of the state, ever more flexibly, to regulate mobility half the world away, it also stretches deeply into the interior, creating within liberal democracies what have been variably referred to as "constitution free" zones or "waiting zones" (*zones d'attente*), where ordinary constitutional rights are partially suspended or limited, especially in relation to those who do not have proper documentation or legal status.[7]

Indeed, making the legal subject wait is one of the key elements of temporal governance, and this can be achieved by means of countdown deadlines through qualification, but it is most obvious in procedural differentiations. Procedural differentiations are meant to regulate access to the law in the first place. Basically, they regulate the pace and therewith the length of the legal procedure. This can lead to long waiting periods, but sudden acceleration can just as well influence access to justice. In scholarly literature, access to the law has often been related to the work of Kafka. Bourdieu refers to *The Trial* as "the model of a social universe dominated by such an absolute and unpredictable power, capable of inducing extreme anxiety by condemning its victim to very strong investment combined with very great insecurity."[8] More explicit reference to waiting is to be found in the parable "Before the Law" (which also appears as a chapter in *The Trial*). This is a story about a landman who waits to be granted access to the law by a gatekeeper. "But the gatekeeper says that he cannot grant him entry at the moment. The man thinks about it and then asks if he will be allowed to come in later on. 'It is possible,' says the gatekeeper, 'but not now.'" The man sits for years before the gate, time and again asking for entrances but the gatekeepers keeps refusing him and after years he dies without every succeeding to enter the law. This story has been related to the relationship between power and time in the sovereign's

[4] G. Hage, "A Not So Multi-sited Ethnography of a Not So Imagined Community," *Anthropological Theory* 5, no. 4 (2005); G. Hage, *Waiting*, MUP Academic Monographs (Carlton: MUP Academic Digital, 2009).

[5] McNevin, "Time and the Figure of the Citizen," p. 547.

[6] A. McNevin and A. Missbach, "Luxury Limbo: Temporal Techniques of Border Control and the Humanitarianisation of Waiting," *International Journal of Migration and Border Studies* 4, nos. 1/2 (2018), p. 17.

[7] Shachar, *The Shifting Border*, p. 6.

[8] Bourdieu, *Pascalian Meditations*, p. 229.

capacity to make migrants wait at borders.[9] In such forms of temporal governance, the human time of the individual is at the heart of this operation of power.

> Waiting implies submission; the interested aiming at something greatly desired duraly – that is to say, for the whole duration of the expectancy – modifies the behaviour of the person who "hangs," as we say, on the awaited decision. It follows that the art of "taking one's time," of "letting time take its time," as Cervantes puts it, of making people wait, of delaying without destroying hope, of adjourning without totally disappointing, which would have the effect of killing the waiting itself, is an integral part of the exercise of power,

Bourdieu writes.[10]

This phenomenon of the shifting border, in which the temporal border is one of the key features, reaffirms precisely the double-edged or Janus-faced role of time in the control of the presence of migrants within a certain territory that I have attempted to demonstrate in this book. On the one hand, the temporal border is the demonstration of the seemingly endless possibilities of the governance of the presence of migrants within a given territory by means of time. The intricate relationship between human time and clock time that is at work in legal time enables all kinds of temporal differentiation, by means of temporality, deadlines, procedures, or qualification. On the other hand, precisely these frenetic attempts to prevent migrants from reaching the territory and the endless efforts to cut down to the bone the entitlement of those present on the territory by means of temporal differentiation demonstrate in a rather cynical way the normative force of the jus temporis that I have argued for in this book. It is because we acknowledge that generally the presence of migrants within a territory matters that we try to prevent people from reaching our territory and that we develop measures that limit those entitlements for the undesired aliens. Similar reasoning applies to the legal differentiation between the physical act of being present within a certain territory and the legal admission to this territory[11] or the disqualification of certain presences as unlawful. It is because we generally acknowledge the value of durable presence within a given territory that we make all sorts of temporal differentiations to exclude certain categories from these entitlements by means of time.

Yet clearly, it leads to further bifurcation of the temporal presence of migrants: some people are followed by the border everywhere and seemingly endlessly, whilst others never encounter any gate or threshold in their smooth mobility. "Being here" has become more and more a limited commodity, both as regards the actual presence within the territory and the legal meaning of such presence. The analysis in this book adds to this discussion, it has focussed on the temporal governance of the presence of migrants within the territory – the temporal governance of "being here." Even though I subscribe to arguments that criticize the "overrated premium of territorial arrival," as Shachar puts it, I have focussed in this

[9] H. van Houtum, "Waiting before the Law: Kafka on the Border," *Social & Legal Studies* 19, no. 3 (2010). Eule et al. have investigated how both border guards and migrant's navigate through the contradictory times of the migration regime. Also they show that these protracted waiting periods were not always the result of conscious policy choices, often bureaucrats simply did not seem to care or think about the implications of "unnecessary dragging out decision-making processes," Eule et al., *Migrants before the Law*, p. 161.

[10] Bourdieu, *Pascalian Meditations*, p. 228.

[11] Shachar, *The Shifting Border*, p. 24; Volpp, "Imaginings of Space in Immigration Law."

book on the legal temporal techniques that enable such a form of exclusion within the territory.[12]

Time is so apt for control because it refers to the process of someone's life within a territory that would otherwise be difficult to grasp. Time is both singular and general, it is objective and subjective, endless and finite, reversible and irreversible, it moves and is fixated, it has succession and exteriority, it is eternal and mortal. I have shown that it is precisely the Janus face of legal time, the space between these different conceptions, that are at work in legal time that makes it so useful for legal control. It is because the clock can be related to the life of a migrant, without it being the same as the human time of the migrant, that it can easily be manipulated for different policy aims. After all, the life of a legal subject can be expressed in clock time and therefore objectified, whilst at the same time, this clock time has meaning in the life of this human being. A detention of one year is not only a means to express the severity of the punishment – with which objectification it is possible to compare to other penalties – this one year is also the lived time of the legal subject. The punishment will be a lived experience that takes human time, time that is finite and irreversible.

The same goes for the use for a temporal technique such as ex nunc or ex tunc assessment in adjudication, to assess a case as if time had not or had lapsed. Such a mechanism is only conceivable because we can make sense of the difference between the actual human time that has lapsed, and cannot be turned back, and refer this actual moment to the time of the clock (i.e. the calendar) that can be traversed forward and backward. Temporality, the conception of time as past, present, and future, presumes a human perspective, one cannot determine simply on the basis of a calendar whether it is the past or the future. It is always someone's past, someone's present, and someone's future. It is in the moment of the legal judgment that time is fixated: a past, present, and future are constructed in order to do justice at that moment. Yet, the problem is, in the words of Thomas van Aquino, that "a variable matter cannot be judged upon before it has come to an end."[13] However, that is precisely what a legal judgment has to do, decide the ongoing matter as if it was Judgment Day, from the perspective as if everything had come to an end and all circumstances of the matter could be overseen and clearly interpreted. Procedures have to come to an end because a decision is demanded. The legal decision must "rend time," as Jacques Derrida puts it, it is an interval in which the streaming character of time has to be halted. The decision should, in other words, be eternal and temporal to be just.

The Janus face of legal time can equally be pinpointed in the qualification of time. Time may be legally irrelevant, unlawful, interrupted, or otherwise legally irrelevant. In such cases, the temporal control is based on the qualification of the *actual* human time that has lapsed or will lapse; it refers to the process of the life of the migrant. The whole point of differentiation presumes that the process that is being differentiated continues, that human time lapses. It is only because the process actually continues that temporal differentiation can be made, and some forms of time on the territory can be disqualified.

It is in the space between these different oppositions of time – most notably, human time and clock time – that makes legal time so apt for usage in law. What is more, it seems as if this temporal manipulation is seemingly without limitation. After all, it is rather easy to

[12] Shachar, *The Shifting Border*, p. 71.

[13] As cited in G. Agamben, *Pilatus & Jezus*, trans. W. Hemelrijk (Amsterdam: Sjibbolet Filosofie, 2014), p. 61, my translation from Dutch.

change a countdown deadline for naturalization from five years into twenty years. Or to stipulate that someone's residence may *never* be regularized or that a residence permit can always be withdrawn. It seems as if the temporal border can follow the migrant forever, or even preclude them from the most basic rights and residence entitlements in the first place. The question arises, however, whether there are legal and normative limitations to such forms of governance? Obviously, many arguments exist on which the (prolonged) inclusion of migrants can be grounded; these can be liberal, communitarian, based on domicile, ties, affiliation, roots, or even money. Additionally, as Cohen has argued, it is precisely one of the values of the use of a certain period of time for asylum procedures, or naturalization for example, that it can simultaneously refer to multiple even contradictory values and arguments.

Yet, I have argued in this book that hidden in the characteristic of human time is yet another argument for inclusion. This argument of jus temporis is grounded in the specific characteristics of human time, being singular, irreversible, finite, and impossible to stop. I argue that this is captured in the notion of rootedness, as the entanglement of presence within a territory with the lapse of finite and irreversible human time. This rootedness is to be distinguished from integration as ground for inclusion, for such is part of a meritocratic form of governance that includes migrants on the basis of a certain qualification of presence over time. Obviously, such a framework has its own value (and clear disadvantages), yet the case of long-term residing migrants who commit crimes shows *in extremis* its exclusionary side.

I have exposed concrete implications of jus temporis that are already at work in European migration law and practice. Basically, these implications boil down to sorts of rules and regulations. First, the temporal governance of the presence of migrants within the territory should *at least* have a moment in time in which the situation is assessed, in which there is a *possibility* for the acquisition of (stronger) residence entitlements. Clearly, this is to be found in being able to acquire long-term residence after five years in EU law, or the prospect of naturalization after a probationary period of time, which is often also five years. The same goes for migrants that unlawfully reside for a long period of time within the territory. They should also at least have the option to regularize their presence after a lapse of time. In many European countries, there are prospects to regularize unlawful presence based on humanitarian considerations, just as many countries use a regularization scheme once in a while to grant a group of migrants residence permits. Nonetheless, the possibility is clearly not the same as the actual inclusion of long-term residing migrants. The critical state of jus temporis in European law is similarly reflected in the way in which these opportunities for acquiring stronger residence rights have been limited.

Second, the threat of exclusion or actual exclusion of long-term residing migrants should be terminated at a certain moment in time. If migrants remain present on a territory over time, the threat of expulsion remains, simply because lawful entry was not available in the first place, or due to legitimate reasons for withdrawal of their residence permit. Yet, this temporal border should be stopped at some point in human time. There should be a moment in which lawfully residing migrants can no longer be expelled, for whatever reason.[14] And the same goes for unlawfully residing migrants, alongside the chance to

[14] In the Netherlands, it was, until 2012 impossible to withdraw a residence permit on the basis of public order after twenty years of lawful residence, no matter what crime the migrant had committed.

regularize at a certain moment, there should simply be a moment in human time when it is possible to receive a residence status, purely on the basis of the "life-time" that has lapsed. I would argue in favor of a similar countdown deadline in procedures, which would counterweight the risk that governments simply decelerate procedures in order to let migrants wait.

As Hannah Arendt argues in *The Human Condition*, just as human life is defined by its mortality, human action is characterized by the capacity to start anew, by natality. "Without being forgiven, released from the consequences of what we have done, our capacity to act would, as it were, be confined to one single deed from which we could never recover; we would remain the victim of its consequences forever."[15] In a way, my argument of jus temporis is stating the obvious: human time has value. Humans are mortal spatiotemporal beings; they are entangled in space and time, and their life is not endless, nor can it be rewound or paused. The protection of human dignity in (human) rights inevitably boils down to the protection of human time and providing human beings the possibility of starting anew. Temporal governance finds it ultimate limitation in the normative value of human time. Migration law that neglects the value of human time is vain.

[15] Arendt, *The Human Condition*, p. 237.

BIBLIOGRAPHY

Adam, B. *Timewatch: The Social Analysis of Time*. Cambridge: Polity Press, 1995.

Time. Cambridge: Polity Press, 2004.

Agamben, G. *Pilatus & Jezus*. Translated by W. Hemelrijk. Amsterdam: Sjibbolet Filosofie, 2014.

The Kingdom and the Garden. London: Seagull Books, 2020.

Alweiss, L. "Heidegger and 'the Concept of Time.'" *History of the Human Sciences* 15, no. 3 (2002): 117–32.

Anderson, B. *Imagined Communities: Reflections on the Origin and Spread of Nationalism*. London: Verso, 2016.

Anderson, B. "And About Time Too . . . Migration Documentation, and Temporalities." In Global Insecurities. Paper Trails: Migrants, Documents, and Legal Insecurity, edited by S. B. Horton and J. Heyman, 53–73. Durham, NC: Duke University Press, 2020.

Anderson, B., M. Griffiths, and A. Rogers. "Migration, Time and Temporalities: Review and Prospect." *Compas Research Resources Paper* (2013). www.compas.ox.ac.uk/wp-content/uploads/RR-2013-Migration_Time_Temporalities.pdf.

Anderson, R. "Time and the Migrant Other: European Border Controls and the Temporal Economics of Illegality." *American Anthropologist* 116, no. 4 (2014): 795–809.

Arendt, H. *The Human Condition*. Chicago: The University of Chicago Press, 1998.

Augustine. *Confessions*. Translated by A. C. Outler. Grand Rapids, MI: Christian Classics Ethereal Library, 1955.

Confessions. Translated by H. Chadwick. Oxford: Oxford University Press, 2009.

Bauböck, R. "Stakeholder Citizenship and Transnational Political Participation: A Normative Evaluation of External Voting." *Fordham Law Review* 75, no. 5 (2007): 2393–447.

"Temporary Migrants, Partial Citizenship and Hypermigration." *Critical Review of International Social and Political Philosophy* 14, no. 5 (2011): 665–93.

"Democratic Inclusion." In *Democratic Inclusion: A Pluralist Theory of Citizenship*. Manchester: Manchester University Press, 2018.

Bauböck, R., E. Ersboll, C. A. Groenendijk, and H. Waldrauch. *Acquisition and Loss of Nationality. Policies and Trends in 15 European States*. Volume 1: Comparative Analyses. Amsterdam: Amsterdam University Press, 2006.

Acquisition and Loss of Nationality. Policies and Trends in 15 European States. Volume 2: Country Analyses. Amsterdam: Amsterdam University Press, 2006.

Bauder, H. "Jus Domicile: In Pursuit of a Citizenship of Equality and Social Justice." *Journal of International Political Theory* 8, nos. 1–2 (2012): 184–96. https://doi.org/10.3366/jipt.2012.0038.

"Domicile Citizenship, Migration and the City." In *Migration Policy and Practice: Interventions and Solutions*, edited by H. Bauder and C. Matheis, 79–101. New York: Palgrave, 2016.

Benhabib, S. *The Rights of Others: Aliens, Residents and Citizens*. Cambridge: Cambridge University Press, 2004.

Bergson, H. *Durée et Simultanitéité*. Paris: Alcan, 1923.

Time and Free Will: An Essay on the Immediate Data of Consciousness. [Essai sur les données immédiates de la conscience]. Translated by F. L. Pogson. New York: Dover Publications, 2001.

Böcker, A., and T. Strik. "Language and Knowledge Tests for Permanent Residence Rights: Help or Hindrance for Integration?" *European Journal of Migration and Law* 13, no. 2 (2011): 157.

Boeles, P., M. den Heijer, G. Lodder, and K. Wouters. *European Migration Law*. Cambridge: Intersentia, 2014.

Bosniak, L. *The Citizen and the Alien*. Princeton, NJ: Princeton University Press, 2006.

"Being Here: Ethical Territoriality and the Rights of Immigrants." *Theoretical Inquiries in Law* 8 no. 2 (2007): 389–410.

"Amnesty in Immigration: Forgetting, Forgiving, Freedom." *Critical Review of International Social and Political Philosophy* 16, no. 3 (2013): 344–65.

"Wrongs, Rights and Regularization." *Moral Philosophy and Politics* 3, no. 2 (2016): 187. https://doi.org/10.1515/mopp-2016-0036. www.degruyter.com/view/journals/mopp/3/2/article-p187.xml.

Bourdieu, P. *Pascalian Meditations*. Translated by R. Nice. Stanford, CA: Stanford University Press, 2000.

Braidotti, R. *Nomadic Subjects*. New York: Columbia University Press, 2011.

Braun, K. "Biopolitics and Temporality in Arendt and Foucault." *Time and Society* 16, no. 1 (2007): 5–23.

Brouwer, E., and R. Lanneau. "Age Assessment and the Protection of Minor Asylum Seekers: Time for a Harmonised Approach in the EU." *Refugee Law Initiative* (2020). https://rli.blogs.sas.ac.uk/2020/08/10/age-assessment-and-the-protection-of-minor-asylum-seekers-time-for-a-harmonised-approach-in-the-eu/.

Brux, C., P. K. Hilden, and A. L. O. Middelthon. "'Klokka Tikker, Tiden Gar': Time and Irregular Migration." *Time and Society* 28, no. 4 (2019): 1429–63.

Çalı, B., and S. Cunningham. "The European Court of Human Rights and Removal of Long-term Migrants." In *Migration and the European Convention on Human Rights*, edited by B. Çalı, L. Bianku, and I. Motoc, 159–74. Oxford: Oxford University Press, 2021.

Carens, J. H. *Immigrants and the Right to Stay*. Cambridge, MA: The MIT Press, 2010.

The Ethics of Immigration. Oxford: Oxford University Press, 2013.

Chowdhury, T. *Time, Temporality and Legal Judgment*. Abingdon: Taylor & Francis Group, 2020.

Cohen, E. F. *Semi-citizenship in Democratic Politics*. Cambridge: Cambridge University Press, 2009.

"Citizenship and the Law of Time in the United States." *Duke Journal of Constitution Law & Public Policy* 53, no. 8 (2013): 53–79.

The Political Value of Time. Cambridge: Cambridge University Press, 2018.

Coope, U. *Time for Aristotle*. Oxford Aristotle Studies. Oxford: Oxford University Press, 2008.

Corrias, L., and L. Francot, eds. *Temporal Boundaries of Law: Time Out of Joint*. London: Routledge, 2018.

Council of Europe. *European Convention on Nationality: Explanatory Report*. Strasbourg: Council of Europe, 1997.

Cwerner, S. B. "The Times of Migration." *Journal of Ethnic and Migration Studies* 27, no. 1 (2001): 7–36.

Dauvergne, C., and S. Marsden. "The Ideology of Temporary Labour Migration in the Post-global Era." *Citizenship Studies* 18, no. 2 (2014): 224–42. https://doi.org/10.1080/13621025.2014.886441.

de Waal, T. M. "Conditional Belonging: Evaluating Integration Requirements from a Social Equality Perspective." *Journal of Intercultural Studies* 41, no. 2 (2020): 231–47. https://doi.org/10.1080/07256868.2020.1724906.

Integration Requirements for Immigrants in Europe: A Legal-Philosophical Inquiry. London: Bloomsbury, 2021.

Deleuze, G., and F. Guattari. *A Thousand Plateaus: Capitalism and Schizophrenia*. Translated by B. Massumi. London: The Athlone Press, 1996.

Dembour, M. B. *When Humans Become Migrants: Study of the European Court of Human Rights with an Inter-American Counterpoint*. Oxford: Oxford University Press, 2015. http://dx.doi.org/10.1093/acprof:oso/9780199667833.001.0001. https://oxford.universitypressscholarship.com/10.1093/acprof:oso/9780199667833.001.0001/acprof-9780199667833.

Derrida, J. *Pardonner: L'impardonnable et l'imprescriptible*. Paris: Éditions Galilée, 2012.

Le Parjure et Le Pardon. Volume 1: Séminaire (1997–1998). Paris: Éditions du Seuil, 2019.

Dummet, M. *On Immigration and Refugees*. London: Routledge, 2001.

Elias, N. *An Essay on Time*. Dublin: University College Dublin Press, 2007.

Eule, T. G., L. M. Borelli, A. Lindberg, and A. Wyss. *Migrants before the Law*. Cham: Palgrave, 2019.

Ghorashi, H. "Negotiating Belonging beyond Rootedness: Unsettling the Sedentary Bias in the Dutch Culturalist Discourse." *Ethnic and Racial Studies* 40, no. 14 (2017): 2426–43. https://doi.org/10.1080/01419870.2016.1248462.

Gibney, M. J. "Should Citizenship Be Conditional? The Ethics of Denationalization." *The Journal of Politics* 75, no. 3 (2013): 646–58. https://doi.org/10.1017/s0022381613000352. www.jstor.org.vu-nl.idm.oclc.org/stable/10.1017/s0022381613000352.

Goodwin-Gill, G. S., and J. McAdam. *The Refugee in International Law.* Oxford: Oxford University Press, 2007.

Grabham, E., and S. Beynon-Jones, eds. *Law and Time.* London: Routledge, 2020.

Greenhouse, C. J. "Just in Time: Temporality and the Cultural Legitimation of Law." *Yale Law Journal* 98 (1989): 1631–52.

Griffiths, M. B. E. "Frenzied, Decelerating and Suspended: The Temporal Uncertainties of Failed Asylum Seekers and Immigration Detainees." *Compas Research Resources Papers*, no. 105 (2013).

"Living with Uncertainty: Indefinite Immigration Detention." *Journal of Legal Anthropology* 1, no. 3 (2013): 263–86.

"Out of Time: The Temporal Uncertainties of Refused Asylum Seekers and Immigration Detainees." *Journal of Ethnic and Migration Studies* 40, no. 12 (2014): 1991–2009.

"The Changing Politics of Time in the UK Immigration System." In *Timespace and International Migration*, edited by E. Mavroudi, A. Christou, and B. Page, 48–60. Camberley: Edward Elgar Publishing, 2017.

Gross, D. "Temporality and the Modern State." *Theory and Society* 14, no. 1 (1985): 53–82. https://doi.org/10.1007/BF00160928.

Guerlac, S. "The Fragility of the Pardon (Derrida and Ricoeur)." In *Derrida and the Time of the Political*, edited by P. Cheah and S. Guerlac, 255–73. Durham, NC: Duke University Press, 2009.

Guild, E., C. A. Groenendijk, and S. Carrera. *Illiberal Liberal States.* Farnham: Ashgate, 2009.

Gündogdu, A. *Rightlessness in an Age of Rights: Hannah Arendt and the Contemporary Struggles of Migrants.* Oxford: Oxford University Press, 2015.

Hage, G. "A Not So Multi-sited Ethnography of a Not So Imagined Community." *Anthropological Theory* 5, no. 4 (2005): 463–75. https://doi.org/10.1177/1463499605059232. https://journals.sagepub.com/doi/abs/10.1177/1463499605059232.

Waiting. MUP Academic Monographs. Carlton: MUP Academic Digital, 2009. https://search.ebscohost.com/login.aspx?direct=true&db=nlebk&AN=2232004&site=ehost-live.

Hambly, J., and N. Gill. "Law and Speed: Asylum Appeals and the Techniques and Consequences of Legal Quickening." *Journal of Law and Society* 47, no. 1 (2020): 3–28. https://doi.org/10.1111/jols.12220. https://onlinelibrary.wiley.com/doi/abs/10.1111/jols.12220.

Hammar, T. "Legal Time of Residence and the Status of Immigrants." In *From Aliens to Citizens: Redefining the Status of Immigrants in Europe*, edited by R. Bauböck, 187–98. Vienna: European Centre, 1994.

Hassan, R. *Empires of Speed: Time and the Acceleration of Politics and Society.* The Hague: Brill, 2009.

Hawking, S. *A Brief History of Time.* New York: Bantam Books, 1995.

Heidegger, M. *The Concept of Time.* New York: John Wiley and Sons, 1991.

Sein und Zeit. Tubingen: Max Niemeyer Verlag, 2006.

Honig, B. *Emergency Politics: Paradox, Law, Democracy.* Princeton, NJ: Princeton University Press, 2009.

Hoy, D. C. *The Time of Our Lives: A Critical History of Temporality.* Cambridge, MA: The MIT Press, 2009.

Ineli-Ciger, M. *Temporary Protection in Law and Practice.* International Refugee Law Series. Leiden: Martinus Nijhoff, 2018. https://login.ezproxy.leidenuniv.nl:2443/login?URL=http://search.ebscohost.com/login.aspx?direct=true&db=e000xww&AN=1660729&site=ehost-live.

"What a Difference Two Decades Make? The Shift from Temporary to Immediate Protection in the New European Pact on Asylum and Migration." *EU Migration Blog* (2020). https://eumigrationlawblog.eu/what-a-difference-two-decades-make-the-shift-from-temporary-to-immediate-protection-in-the-new-european-pact-on-asylum-and-migration/.

Jacobsen, C. M., M.-A. Karlsen, and S. Khosravi, eds. *Waiting and the Temporalities of Irregular Migration.* London: Routledge, 2020.

Kasparek, B., "Routes, Corridors, and Spaces of Exception: Governing Migration and Europe." *Near Futures Online 1 "Europe at a Crossroads"* (2016). http://nearfuturesonline.org/routes-corridors-and-spaces-of-exception-governing-migration-and-europe/.

Khosravi, S. "Waiting." In *A COMPAS Anthology*, edited by B. Anderson and M. Keith, 74. Oxford: COMPAS, 2014.

Klinke, I. "Chronopolitics: A Conceptual Matrix." *Progress in Human Geography* 37, no. 5 (2012): 673–90.

Kobelinski, C. *L'accueil des demandeurs d'asile: Une ethnographie de l'attente.* Paris: Éditions du Cygne, 2010.

Kostakopoulou, D. *The Future Governance of Citizenship*. Law in Context. Cambridge: Cambridge University Press, 2008.

Kroeze, H. "Distinguishing between Use and Abuse of EU Free Movement Law: Evaluating Use of the 'Europe-Route' for Family Reunification to Overcome Reverse Discrimination." In *European Citizenship under Stress*, edited by N. Cambien, D. Kochenov, and E. Muir, 222–70. Leiden: Martinus Nijhoff, 2020.

Kroeze, H., and P. van Elsuwege. "Revisiting Ruiz Zambrano: A Never Ending Story?" *European Journal of Migration and Law* 23, no. 1 (2021): 1–12. https://doi.org/10.1163/15718166-12340091. https://brill.com/view/journals/emil/23/1/article-p1_1.xml.

Lefebvre, A. *The Image of Law*. Stanford, CA: Stanford University Press, 2008.

"The Time of Law: Evolution in Holmes and Bergson." In *Deleuze and Law: Forensic Futures*, edited by R. Braidotti, C. Colebrook, and P. Hanafin, 24–46. London: Palgrave Macmillan, 2009.

"Human Rights in Deleuze and Bergson's Later Philosophy." In *Deleuze and Law*, edited by L. de Sutter and K. McGee, 48–68. Edinburgh: Edinburgh University Press, 2012.

Levinson, A. *The Regularisation of Unauthorized Migrants: Literature Survey and Country Case Studies*. Oxford: COMPAS, 2005. www.compas.ox.ac.uk/2005/er-2005-regularisation_unauthorized_literature/.

Lippincott, K., U. Eco, and E. H. Gombrich. *The Story of Time*. London: Merrell Publishers, 2003.

Lori, N. "Migration, Time and the Shift to Autocracy." In *The Shifting Border*, edited by A. Shachar and P. Niesen, 118–38. Manchester: Manchester University Press, 2020.

Maas, W. "Unauthorized Migration and the Politics of Regularization, Legalization, and Amnesty." In *Labour Migration in Europe*, edited by G. Menz and A. Caviedes, 232–50. London: Palgrave Macmillan, 2010.

Macklin, A., and R. Bauböck. "The Return of Banishment: Do the New Denationalisation Policies Weaken Citizenship?" *EUI Working Paper*, RSCAS 2015/14 (2015).

Malkki, L. "National Geographic: The Rooting of Peoples and the Territorialization of National Identity among Scholars and Refugees." *Cultural Anthropology* 7, no. 1 (1992): 24–44. www.jstor.org.vu-nl.idm.oclc.org/stable/656519.

Mantu, S. "Concepts of Time and European Citizenship." *European Journal of Migration and Law* 15, no. 4 (2013): 447–64. https://doi.org/10.1163/15718166-00002044. https://brill.com/view/journals/emil/15/4/article-p447_5.xml.

McNevin, A. "Time and the Figure of the Citizen." *International Journal of Politics, Culture, and Society* 33 (2020): 545–59. https://doi.org/10.1007/s10767-020-09358-4.

McNevin, A., and A. Missbach. "Luxury Limbo: Temporal Techniques of Border Control and the Humanitarianisation of Waiting." *International Journal of Migration and Border Studies* 4, nos. 1/2 (2018): 12–34.

McTaggart, J. E. "The Unreality of Time." *Mind: A Quarterly Review of Psychology and Philosophy* 17 (1908): 456–73.

Miller, D. *Strangers in Our Midst: The Political Philosophy of Immigration*. Cambridge, MA: Harvard University Press, 2016.

Motomura, H. "We Asked for Workers but Families Came: Time, Law and the Family in Immigration and Citizenship." *Virginia Journal of Social Policy & the Law* 14, no. 1 (2006): 103–18.

Muldoon, M. "Time, Self, and Meaning in the Works of Henri Bergson, Maurice Merleau-Ponty, and Paul Ricoeur." *Philosophy Today* 35, no. 3 (1991): 254–68.

Nail, T. *The Figure of the Migrant*. Stanford, CA: Stanford University Press, 2015.

Nietzsche, F. *De Geboorte van de Tragedie of Griekse Cultuur en Pessimisme*. Translated by H. Driessen. Amsterdam: De Arbeiderspers, 2009.

Ochoa Espejo, P. "Taking Place Seriously: Territorial Presence and the Rights of Immigrants." *The Journal of Political Philosophy* 24, no. 1 (2016): 67–87.

Ost, F. *Le Temps du Droit*. Paris: Editions Odile Jacob, 1999.

Peroni, L. "*Paposhvili* v. *Belgium*: Memorable Grand Chamber Judgment Reshapes Article 3 Case Law on Expulsion of Seriously Ill Persons." *Strasbourg Observers* (2016). https://strasbourgobservers.com/2016/12/15/paposhvili-v-belgium-memorable-grand-chamber-judgment-reshapes-article-3-case-law-on-expulsion-of-seriously-ill-persons/.

Pilgram, L. "International Law and European Nationality Laws." *EUDO Citizenship Policy Brief* (2011). https://cadmus.eui.eu/bitstream/handle/1814/19455/EUDO_CIT_2011_01_Pilgram.pdf?sequence=1.

Postill, J. "Clock and Calendar Time: A Missing Anthropological Problem." *Time & Society* 11, nos. 2/3 (2002): 251–70.

Ranchordás, S., and Y. Roznai, eds. *Time, Law and Change: An Interdisciplinary Study.* London: Hart Publishers, 2020.

Reijven, J., and J. van Wijk. "Caught in Limbo: How Alleged Perpetrators of International Crimes Who Applied for Asylum in the Netherlands Are Affected by a Fundamental System Error in International Law." *International Journal of Refugee Law* 26, no. 2 (2014): 248–71.

Reneman, A. M., and M. C. Stronks. "What Are They Waiting For? The Use of Acceleration and Deceleration in Asylum Procedures by the Dutch Government." *Time & Society* 30, no. 3 (2021): 302–31. https://doi.org/10.1177/0961463x211006053. https://journals.sagepub.com/doi/abs/10.1177/0961463X211006053.

Ricoeur, P. *Time and Narrative.* Volume 1. Chicago: The University of Chicago Press, 1984.

Time and Narrative. Volume 3. Chicago: The University of Chicago Press, 1988.

The Just. Chicago: The University of Chicago Press, 2000.

Memory, History, Forgetting. Chicago: The University of Chicago Press, 2004.

Robertson, S. "Time and Temporary Migration: The Case of Temporary Graduate Workers and Working Holiday Makers in Australia." *Journal of Ethnic and Migration Studies* 40, no. 12 (2014): 1915–33. https://doi.org/10.1080/1369183X.2013.876896.

Rosa, H. *Resonanz: Eine Soziologie der Weltbeziehung.* Frankfurt: Suhrkamp Verlag GmbH, 2016.

Rotter, R. "Waiting in the Asylum Determination Process: Just an Empty Interlude." *Time and Society* 25, no. 1 (2016): 80–101.

Rubio-Marín, R. *Immigration as a Democratic Challenge: Citizenship and Inclusion in Germany and the United States.* Cambridge: Cambridge University Press, 2000.

Ryan, B. "Selective Citizenship: How the Court of Justice Linked Security of Residence to Integration." *European Journal of Migration and Law* 21, no. 3 (2019): 374–99.

Sandel, M. J. *The Tyranny of Merit: What Becomes of the Common Good.* London: Allen Lane, 2020.

Schinkel, W. *Imagined Societies : A Critique of Immigrant Integration in Western Europe.* Cambridge: Cambridge University Press, 2017.

Schopenhauer, A. *Die Welt Als Wille und Vorstellung.* Munich: Deutscher Taschenbuch Verlag GmbH & Co., 1998.

Schwartz, B. "Waiting, Exchange, and Power: The Distribution of Time in Social Systems." *American Journal of Sociology* 79, no. 4 (1974): 841–70.

Severson, E. *Levinas's Philosophy of Time.* Pittsburgh: Duquesne University Press, 2013.

Shachar, A. *The Birthright Lottery.* Cambridge, MA: Harvard University Press, 2009.

"Earned Citizenship: Property Lessons for Immigration Reform." *Yale Journal of Law and the Humanities* 23, no. 1 (2011): 110–58.

"Selecting by Merit: The Brave New World of Stratified Mobility." In *Migration in Political Theory*, 175–204. Oxford: Oxford University Press, 2016.

"Citizenship for Sale?" In *The Oxford Handbook of Citizenship*, edited by A. Shachar, R. Bauböck, I. Bloemraad, and M. Vink, 789–816. Oxford: Oxford University Press, 2017.

The Shifting Border: Legal Cartographies of Migration and Mobility. Manchester: Manchester University Press 2020.

Somek, A. "Solidarity Decomposed: Being and Time in European Citizenship." University of Iowa Legal Studies Research Paper, nos. 7–13 (2007).

Song, S. "The Significance of Territorial Presence and the Rights of Immigrants." In *Migration in Political Theory*, 225–48. Oxford: Oxford University Press, 2016.

"The Rights of Noncitizens in the Territory." In *Immigration and Democracy*, 173–88. New York: Oxford University Press, 2018.

Sonnema, R. B. *The Early Dutch Vanitas Still-Life.* Michigan: University Microfilms Internationals, 1980.

Spaventa, E. "Family Rights for Circular Migrants and Frontier Workers : O and B, and S and G." *Common Market Law Review* 52, no. 3 (2015): 753–77. http://dro.dur.ac.uk/14874/.

Spijkerboer, T. P. "The Global Mobility Infrastructure: Reconceptualising the Externalisation of Migration Control." *European Journal of Migration and Law* 20, no. 4 (2018): 452.

Steinorth, C. "Üner v the Netherlands: Expulsion of Long-Term Immigrants and the Right to Respect for Private and Family Life." *Human Rights Law Review* 8, no. 1 (2008): 185–96.

Stronks, M. C. "Een Bijna Ongebrijdelde Beteugeling van de Tijd: Een Analyse van Aanscherpingen van de Glijdende Schaal." *Nederlands Juristenblad*, no. 34 (2013): 2306–14.

Talmon, S. "The Constitutive versus the Declaratory Theory of Recognition: Tertium non Datur?" *The British Year Book of International Law* 75, no. 1 (2005): 101–81.

Tazzioli, M. "The Temporal Borders of Asylum: Temporality of Control in the EU Border Regime." *Political Geography* 64, no. 15 (2018): 13–22.

Thym, D. "Residence as de Facto Citizenship? Protection of Long-Term Residence under Article 8 ECHR." In *Human Rights and Immigration*, 106–44. Oxford: Oxford University Press, 2014.

United Nations High Commissioner for Refugees. *Handbook and Guidelines on Procedures and Criteria for Determining Refugee Status*. Geneva: United Nations High Commissioner for Refugees, 2011.

van Houtum, H. "Waiting before the Law: Kafka on the Border." *Social & Legal Studies* 19, no. 3 (2010): 285–97. https://doi.org/10.1177/0964663910372180. https://journals.sagepub.com/doi/abs/10.1177/0964663910372180.

van Oers, R., E. Ersboll, and D. Kostakopoulou. *A Re-definition of Belonging*. Leiden: Martinus Nijhoff, 2009.

van Oort, H. "De Strafrechtelijk Veroordeelde Vreemdeling en Artikel 8 EVRM." *Asiel&Migrantenrecht*, no. 5 (2020): 220–5.

van Walsum, S. K. *The Family and the Nation: Dutch Family Migration Policies in the Context of Changing Family Norms*. Newcastle upon Tyne: Cambridge Scholars Publishing, 2008.

Intimate Strangers. Migration Law Series. Amsterdam: Vrije Universiteit Amsterdam, 2012. www.rechten.vu.nl/en/Images/Walsum_-_Intimate_Strangers_final_tcm248-748831_tcm248-748831.pdf.

Volpp, L. "Imaginings of Space in Immigration Law." *Law, Culture and the Humanities* 9, no. 3 (2013): 456–74. https://doi.org/10.1177/1743872111435963. https://journals.sagepub.com/doi/abs/10.1177/1743872111435963.

Walker, N. "Denizenship and Deterritorialisation in the European Union." In A Right to Inclusion and Exclusion? Normative Fault Lines of the EU's Area of Freedom, Security and Justice, edited by H. Lindahl, 261–72. London: Hart Publishers, 2009.

Walzer, M. *Spheres of Justice*. New York: Basic Books, 1983.

Wyss, A. "Stuck in Mobility? Interrupted Journeys of Migrants with Precarious Legal Status in Europe." *Journal of Immigrant & Refugee Studies* 17, no. 1 (2019): 77–93.

INDEX

www.ingramcontent.com/pod-product-compliance
Lightning Source LLC
Chambersburg PA
CBHW060006290425
25870CB00009B/766
* 9 7 8 1 0 0 9 4 8 4 0 4 6 *